Key
Words
of the
Christian Life

Clearview Baptist Church
6730 Dogwood Rd.
Woodlawn, MD. 21207

Other titles by Warren W. Wiersbe

The 20 Qualities of an Authentic Christian
Be Myself
The Bible Exposition Commentary: New Testament (2 vols.)
The Bumps Are What You Climb On
The Cross of Jesus: What His Words from Calvary Mean for Us
Elements of Preaching
God Isn't in a Hurry: Learning to Slow Down and Live
The Intercessory Prayer of Jesus: Priorities for Dynamic Christian Living
Living with the Giants: The Lives of Great Men of the Faith
The Names of Jesus
On Being a Servant of God
Prayer, Praise, and Promises: A Daily Walk through the Psalms
Run with the Winners
The Strategy of Satan
Turning Mountains into Molehills: And Other Devotional Talks
Victorious Christians You Should Know
Wiersbe's Expository Outlines on the New Testament
Wiersbe's Expository Outlines on the Old Testament

Titles in the Living Lessons from God's Word Series:
Angry People
Caring People
Lonely People

Key Words

of the
Christian Life

UNDERSTANDING
AND APPLYING
THEIR MEANINGS

Warren W. Wiersbe

Baker Books

A Division of Baker Book House Co
Grand Rapids, Michigan 49516

Published by Baker Books
a division of Baker Book House Company
P.O. Box 6287, Grand Rapids, MI 49516-6287

Printed in the United States of America

Library of Congress Cataloging-in-Publication Data

Wiersbe, Warren W.
    Key words of the Christian life / Warren W. Wiersbe.
        p.   cm.
    ISBN 0-8010-6431-7 (pbk.)
    1. Theology, Doctrinal—Popular works. 2. Christian life—Biblical teaching. 3. Bible—Theology. I. Title.
    BT77 .W487 2002
    230′.03—dc21   2002006730

For current information about all releases from Baker Book House, visit our web site:
http://www.bakerbooks.com

Contents

Preface

This book contains edited and expanded transcriptions of radio messages I delivered over the Back to the Bible international network.

These messages were first spoken to a listening audience made up of a variety of people in many nations and at many stages of spiritual growth. This explains the brevity, simplicity, and directness of the material. Were I writing a commentary or presenting a longer pulpit message, the approach would be vastly different.

In sending out these messages, my prayer is that they will encourage and build up God's people and help them in their own ministries.

WARREN W. WIERSBE

The Power of Bible Words

IN 1924 Adolf Hitler started writing his book *Mein Kampf,* which means "My Struggle." Some people ignored the book, and some laughed at it, but for every word in *Mein Kampf,* 125 people died in World War II. Never underestimate the power of words. A judge speaks, and a prisoner is condemned or set free. A physician speaks, and a person has surgery or goes home from the hospital. A government official speaks, and millions of dollars are spent or withheld.

In our own personal lives, we know the power of words—words that can bless us and words that can hurt us. It is very important for us as Christians to know the meaning of Bible words. We need to understand what these words mean and how they apply to our lives. Words such as justification, sanctification, propitiation, imputation, and mediation—these words make up the technical vocabulary of the Christian life and are very important.

Our younger son is an electronics engineer, who designs those little chips that run computers. He had to learn a special vocabulary to do his job. My two older brothers were involved in mechanics, and they could run machines and fix things. They also had to learn a special vocabulary in order to do their jobs. I'm a pastor, a Bible teacher. I had to learn a special vocabulary to be able to study and teach the Word of God.

Some Christians say, "Don't bother me with doctrine; just give me the beautiful devotional thoughts of the Bible." But if devotion is not based upon correct doctrine, it is not going to accomplish anything. It is merely shallow sentiment. In this first chapter I would like to explain why it is important for us to understand these key words of the Christian life.

The reason is very simple: When we understand these words, we are able to live what they teach. When we understand these key words of the Christian life, then we know what a Christian is, what God has done for us, and what God *wants* to do for us.

GOD'S WORD IS LIGHT

Perhaps the best way to approach this would be to introduce some of the pictures of the Word of God found in the Bible. When we understand what God compares His Word to, then we'll know how important it is for us to know the meaning of Bible words and how they apply to our lives.

Let's begin with a very familiar picture of the Word of God—God's Word is light. "Your word is a lamp to my feet and a light for my path" (Ps. 119:105). What does a light do? A light enables us to see. When we understand these key words in the Bible, they are like lamps that guide us throughout all Scripture and throughout the Christian life.

God has revealed truth to us in words. "We have not received the spirit of the world but the Spirit who is from God, that we may understand what God has freely given us. This is what we speak, not in words taught us by human wisdom but in words taught by the Spirit, expressing spiritual truths in spiritual words" (1 Cor. 2:12–13). In other words, God has revealed these things to us in words.

Revelation is simply God's work in communicating truth to us, truth that we could not discover any other way. Sometimes God revealed His truth in dreams or in visions; sometimes people heard a voice; sometimes they saw God in action. We today have God's Word, and we have God's words in the Bible. God has revealed His truth to us that we might know the things that are freely given to us of God.

These words in the Bible are inspired words. Inspiration is the supernatural work of the Holy Spirit in the lives of the writers of the Bible, enabling them to produce a trustworthy, written revelation. "All Scripture is God-breathed and is useful for teaching, rebuking, correcting and training in righteousness, so that the man of God may be thoroughly equipped for every good work" (2 Tim. 3:16–17). Inspiration means that the Holy Spirit of God so worked upon the writers of the Scriptures that they wrote a trustworthy revelation from God.

Second Peter 1:20–21 adds something to this: "Above all, you must understand that no prophecy of Scripture came about by the prophet's own interpretation. For prophecy never had its origin in the will of man, but men spoke from God as they were carried along by the Holy Spirit." The Holy Spirit of God has given to us a dependable, trustworthy revelation of God in the Holy Scriptures, and God has revealed Himself through words.

In 2 Peter 2:3 we have a warning about false prophets and false teachers: "In their greed these teachers will exploit you with stories they have made up." "Stories they have made up" means counterfeit words. The Greek word gives us our English word plastic. Peter warned us about "plastic words." What are plastic words? Words that you can twist around to mean anything. False prophets and false teachers like to use our Christian vocabulary, but they do not use our Christian dictionary. They will talk about salvation, being born again, and being justified and use the words that we use, but they don't use the same meaning. They twist words around to mean what they want them to mean in order to make merchandise out of you. You must be very, very careful of these religious counterfeits who are out to get something out of you instead of put something into you from the Lord. And they do it with plastic words.

God's Word is light; it enables us to see. If you want to know what's really going on in your life, in your world, then you'd better study the words in your Bible.

GOD'S WORD IS FOOD

Second, God's Word is not only light, but God's Word is food. "Jesus answered, 'It is written: "Man does not live on bread alone, but on every word that comes from the mouth of God"'" (Matt. 4:4). Food enables us to grow. As you grow in your knowledge of the Word of God, you can grow in your Christian life. "But grow in the grace and knowledge of our Lord and Savior Jesus Christ" (2 Peter 3:18).

It is possible to grow in knowledge and not grow in grace. I have met people who have a great deal of Bible knowledge, but nobody can get along with them. They run from church to church, creating problems and trying to be important. It is possible to grow in knowledge but not grow in grace; however, when we are growing in knowledge, taught by the Holy Spirit, then we have to grow in grace. The same Holy Spirit who wrote the Word of God writes the Word of God in our hearts (see 2 Cor. 3:1–3) and enables us to reveal the fruit of the Spirit.

It is so important for us to grow by feeding on the Word of God. When you understand Bible doctrine—what it means to be justified, what it means to be sanctified, what propitiation means—and appropriate the truth into your own life, then you grow and mature in your Christian life. We read in Jeremiah 15:16, "When your words came, I ate them." Job said, "I have treasured the words of his mouth more than my daily bread" (Job 23:12). In Hebrews 5:11–14 we are told that God's Word is milk and meat. And so we need God's Word as a light to guide us and as food to nourish us.

GOD'S WORD IS A TOOL

Third, God's Word is a tool for building. "'Is not my word like fire,' declares the LORD, 'and like a hammer that breaks a rock in pieces?'" (Jer. 23:29). Sometimes God's Word has to break down before it can build up. Sometimes God's Word has to burn before it can warm. But God's Word is like a hammer—it is a tool for breaking down the old life and building up the new life. It enables us to build the church. Paul said, "Now I commit you to God and to the word of his grace, which can build you up and give you an inheritance among all those who are sanctified" (Acts 20:32). If you want to build your life, you must use tools, and the greatest tool of all is the Word of God. The better you understand the meaning of key Bible words, the more tools you will have in your "spiritual workshop" for building your own Christian life and helping to build the church.

Church history proves that when the Word of God was given its free course, when there was faithful preaching and teaching of the Word of God, the church grew with a strong missionary and evangelistic outreach.

The Word of God is light; it enables us to see. The Word of God is food; it enables us to grow. The Word of God is a tool; it enables us to build.

GOD'S WORD IS A WEAPON

The Word of God is also a weapon; it enables us to fight. Hebrews 4:12 tells us that the Word of God is "living and active." It is "sharper than any double-edged sword." Ephesians 6:17 reminds us that the Word of God is the sword of the Spirit: "Take the helmet of salvation and the sword of the Spirit, which is the word of God." You have discovered that the Christian life is not a playground; it is a battleground. There are false prophets and false teachers around us. There are false religions trying to make merchandise of us. Satan is out to get us. The world is out to get us. Satan is a liar, but God is the one who gives us truth.

It is important that you and I understand the words in the Word of God as weapons to fight battles. When Satan comes with one of his lies and tries to tell you that you have lost your salvation, you will be able to refute him. When you go through a period of despondency and discouragement, you will be able to reach into your armory of weapons and fight the devil.

If doctors, lawyers, and engineers have to learn a technical vocabulary to do their jobs, how much more important it is for us who have eternity in view! How much more important it is for us trying to win lost souls to know these Bible words and use them the way God wants us to use them.

My prayer is that these studies of Bible words will give all of us more light. I trust we will grow as we receive spiritual food and that we will lay hold of the tools and weapons for building and battling. It is my heart's desire that you and I will grow in our spiritual intelligence as we understand the meaning of Bible words.

The Meaning and Method
of Justification

LET'S GO BACK some four thousand years. We see a man sitting on an ash heap. His name is Job. He has a controversy with God because he doesn't quite understand what is going on, why he should be going through so much difficulty.

There are hundreds of questions in the Book of Job, but the most important of all those questions is found in Job 9:2: "How can a mortal be righteous before God?"

Now let's move up to the fall of the year 1515. An Augustinian monk is lecturing on the Book of Romans, and one verse comes to him with great power: "The righteous will live by faith" (1:17). This was the beginning of change in Martin Luther's life and the beginning of the Reformation.

Now move up to May 24, 1738. An Anglican missionary (who wasn't sure of his own salvation) wrote these words in his journal: "In the evening I went very unwillingly to a society in Aldersgate Street where one was reading Luther's Preface to the Epistle to the Romans. About a quarter before nine while he was describing the change which God works in the heart through faith in Christ, I felt my heart strangely warmed. I felt I did trust in Christ, Christ alone for salvation, and assurance was given me that He had taken away my sins, even mine, and saved me from the law of sin and death." And thus did John Wesley receive the assurance of salvation through faith in Christ.

How can a man be just before God? *Justification* is one of the key words in the Christian life. The key verse is Romans 5:1: "Therefore, since we have been justified through faith, we have peace with God through our Lord Jesus Christ." We want to consider justification from three different aspects: the meaning of justification, the method of justification, and the marks of justification.

THE MEANING OF JUSTIFICATION

Justification is the gracious act of God in declaring righteous the sinner who believes on Jesus Christ. You should memorize this definition because it is important.

Justification Is an Act

Notice, please, that justification is an act, not a process. No Christian is more justified than any other Christian. If you are saved and your sister is saved, your sister and you are justified in the same way, and you have the same righteousness. Justification is not a process; it is an act. Instantly, the believer is given a righteous standing before God. It is the gracious act of God, not something that men do. No amount of self-effort or good works could ever bring a person to justification. We do not justify ourselves; it is God who justifies us.

Justification Is Unchanging

Something else is true: Justification is unchanging. Once God has declared that we are righteous through Jesus Christ, the sin question is settled once and for all.

Justification is not the same as regeneration. (We will be talking about regeneration in a later chapter.) Regeneration means being born again. Regeneration gives us new life; justification gives us a new standing before God. Even a newborn baby has a legal standing before the law. Justification gives us a right standing before God; we are accepted in Jesus Christ.

Nor is justification the same as forgiveness. If God forgives me, and I go out and sin again, then I need to be forgiven again. But justification settles things permanently, eternally.

Nor is justification the same as pardon. A pardoned criminal is still a criminal. There is a record of his crimes in a file. Justification removes the guilt and changes our standing. This sounds remarkable, but it's true. Justification means not only that God forgets our sins—past, present, and future—but that God forgets we were ever sinners. He never again treats us as sinners. We are not pardoned criminals; we are not people who have only been forgiven. It is true that pardon is a part of the Christian life, and so is forgiveness; but justification deals with the sin problem once and for all, giving us a right standing before God.

Illustration of Justification

My friend Dr. Roy Gustafson has the finest illustration of justification I have ever heard: There was a man in England who put his Rolls-Royce on the ferryboat and went across to the Continent on a holiday. While he was driving around Europe, something happened to the motor of his car. He cabled the Rolls-Royce people back in England and asked, "I'm having trouble with my car; what do you suggest I do?" Well, the Rolls-Royce people flew a mechanic over! The mechanic repaired the car and flew back to England, leaving the man to continue his holiday. As you can imagine, the fellow was wondering, *How much is this going to cost me?* So when he got back to England, he wrote a letter and asked how much he owed them. He received a letter from the office that read: "Dear Sir: There is no record anywhere in our files that anything ever went wrong with a Rolls-Royce." Now that's justification!

The devil accuses you, you accuse yourself, maybe your friends accuse you; but God checks the file and says, "There is no record anywhere in this file that My child ever did anything wrong." That is justification—the gracious act of God in declaring righteous one who believes in Jesus Christ.

THE METHOD OF JUSTIFICATION

What is the method of justification? How can a holy God justify sinners? How can a holy God overlook sin? Well, God does *not* overlook sin; God deals with it. There are four phrases you want to mark in your Bible in the Book of Romans that explain to us the method of justification.

Freely by His Grace

Romans 3:24 says, "justified freely by his grace." How is God able to justify us? He justifies us by grace, not by merit. The word *freely* is translated "without reason" in John 15:25.

We are "justified without reason by his grace." There is nothing in us that makes God want to justify us. Justification is purely an act of God's grace. Grace means favor that is not deserved and cannot be earned.

God justifies *the wicked.* Romans 4:5 says, "However, to the man who does not work but trusts God who justifies the wicked, his faith is credited as righteousness." In the Old Testament, God warned all the judges that they should justify the righteous and condemn the wicked. Consider Deuteronomy 25:1: "When men have a dispute, they are to take it to court and the judges will decide the case, acquitting the innocent and condemning the guilty." If God did that to you and me, we would all be condemned forever. Why is it that God justifies the ungodly? For the simple reason that there are no *godly* people. "All have sinned and fall short of the glory of God" (Rom. 3:23).

By Faith

Romans 3:28 says, "For we maintain that a man is justified by faith apart from observing the law." Not only are we justified by grace, but we are justified by faith. Whenever you have grace, you must have faith. Whenever you have law, you have to have works. A person cannot be justified by keeping the law. Romans 3:20 states, "Therefore no one will be declared righteous in his sight by observing the law; rather, through the law we become conscious of sin."

We are justified by faith—faith in Christ, faith that comes from the heart. Faith is only as good as the object. Whatever you believe in may be wrong, no matter how sincere you are. Faith in a lie is false security; faith in the truth is saving faith. We are justified by faith, not by works; and we are justified by grace, not by human merit.

By His Blood

Romans 5:9 says, "Since we have now been justified by his blood, how much more shall we be saved from God's wrath through him!" Not only are we justified by grace and by faith, but we are justified by His blood. Somebody has to pay the price for sin. Justification is not some sort of fictional thing where God says, "I'll close my eyes and forget that they have sinned." God in His holiness must deal with sin. In order for God to justify the ungodly, He has to deal with their ungodliness. In order for us to be justified by faith, there has to be a Savior for us to believe in. We are justified by His blood.

Romans 4:25, talking about our Lord Jesus, says, "He was delivered over to death for our sins and was raised to life for our justification." Jesus died on the cross for our sins. He bore the penalty. Now God can be just and the justifier of those who believe in Christ.

The devil comes and says, "How in the world can you declare Warren Wiersbe righteous?" And the answer comes, "By the blood of Jesus Christ." But what about Warren Wiersbe's sins? Jesus Christ died for those sins, and they have been taken care of. We are justified by grace, not by human merit; we are justified by faith, not by works of the law; we are justified by His blood because Christ died for us.

Unto Life

Finally, Romans 5:18 says, "Consequently, just as the result of one trespass was condemnation for all men, so also the result of one act of righteousness was justification that brings life for all men." That's a marvelous phrase—a justification that results in life. We are justified unto life.

Justification is not just something God records in His books. Justification results in a new standing and a new life. That new life is the result of regeneration. But justification makes possible our union with Christ, and this union is described in Romans 5:1–5. It is a life of peace and glory and joy.

Have you put your faith in Jesus Christ? What are you trusting? You say, "I am trusting my church." That will not save you. "I am trusting my good works." That will not save you. We are justified by grace, not by human merit. We are justified by faith, not by works of the law, including religious works. We are justified by His blood; He paid the price. This is a justification of life; we enter into a whole new life. And in our next chapter we will examine the marks of justification and see what happens to the life of the person who trusts Jesus.

The Marks of Justification

WE ARE STUDYING together the key words of the Christian life, the doctrinal words in the Bible that spell out what Christ has done for us and what He wants to do for us today. We began with a study of justification. Justification is the gracious act of God whereby He declares the believing sinner righteous in Christ. We have discussed the meaning of justification. It is an act, not a process; it is the act of God, not something that man does. And God's act justifies a person once and for all.

We also studied the method of justification. Justification is by grace, not by human merit. It is by faith and not by works—even religious works. It is by the blood of Jesus Christ, for He had to die so that our sins might be forgiven. And justification is unto life. It is not separated from life; it changes our lives.

Now we want to look at the marks of justification, and our key passage is Romans 5:1–5:

Therefore, since we have been justified through faith, we have peace with God through our Lord Jesus Christ, through whom we have gained access by faith into this grace in which we now stand. And we rejoice in the hope of the glory of God. Not only so, but we also rejoice in our sufferings, because we know that suffering produces perseverance; perseverance, character; and character, hope. And hope does not disappoint us, because God has poured out his love into our hearts by the Holy Spirit, whom he has given us.

The marks of justification in the believer's life are revealed in relationships. If you are truly justified by faith, then you are going to have a right relationship with God, a right relationship to circumstances, and a right relationship to other people.

RELATIONSHIP WITH GOD

Let's begin with this right relationship with God described in Romans 5:1–2. You will recall that justification has to do with our standing before God. Justification does not *make* people righteous; they are *declared* righteous. Now the consequence of this, of course, is a righteous life. The person who claims he or she is justified by faith but who lives a godless life is declaring that their lips are lying. Justification before God results in a changed life that is visible to other people.

Peace with God

Notice first of all that we have peace with God. "Therefore, since we have been justified through faith, we have peace with God through our Lord Jesus Christ" (Rom. 5:1). When we were unsaved, we were at war with God. "For if, when we were God's enemies, we were reconciled to him through the death of his Son, how much more, having been reconciled, shall we be saved through his life!" (v. 10). There was a time when you and I were at enmity with God. In fact, Romans 8:7 informs us that the carnal mind, the fleshly mind, is at enmity with God. The person who has never been born again doesn't think God's thoughts and doesn't desire what God desires; therefore, he is at war with God.

We cannot have peace until we first have righteousness. Justification has to do with righteousness. Because Jesus Christ died on the cross and rose again, we can have His righteousness when we put our faith in Him. In Psalm 85:10 we have this statement: "Love and faithfulness meet together; righteousness and peace kiss each other." Righteousness and peace "kiss each other" through Jesus Christ. As sinners, we have no righteousness of our own. Our righteousness before God is as filthy rags (see Isa. 64:6). But when we receive His mercy—when we believe His truth—then righteousness is placed on our account. We are justified; therefore, we have peace. There can be no peace without righteousness.

The prophet Isaiah makes this very clear in Isaiah 32:17: "The fruit of righteousness will be peace; the effect of righteousness will be quietness and confidence forever." So the first mark of justification, as far as my relationship to God is concerned, is that I have peace with God. I am not afraid of Him, although I have a reverence for Him. I am not at war with Him. I have a peace in my heart that comes from a clear conscience, a clean heart, a righteous standing before God.

Access to God

Second, not only is there peace with God, but there is access to God. We have peace with God through our Lord Jesus Christ, "through whom we have gained access by *faith* into this grace in which we now stand" (Rom. 5:2). The unsaved person has no open access to God because he has no standing before God. Those who have been justified by faith have access to God through the Lord Jesus Christ. We can come to the throne of grace, we can talk to our heavenly Father, and we can fellowship with Him.

This access is into grace. "We have gained access by faith into this grace in which we now stand" (Rom. 5:2). Our standing before God is one of grace and not one of law. Grace means that God provides for us; law means we try in our own strength to live to please God. Grace means God's Resources Available to Christians Everywhere or God's Riches At Christ's Expense. When you come by faith in Christ, you have access into the grace of God.

It is a marvelous thing to know that you are living by grace and not by law. You are not living by your own merit or by your own ability; you are living by the grace of God that is sufficient for everything.

Hope in the Glory of God

We not only have peace with God and access to God, but we rejoice in hope of the glory of God. Unsaved people have no hope, no future about which they can rejoice. When you trust Christ as your Savior, you are standing in grace, and you are rejoicing in hope. You have a bright future ahead of you because you are justified by faith.

What is this hope? The glory of God! Romans 3:23 informs us that all have sinned and fall short of the glory of God. None of us measures up to God's glory. But when you become a Christian and are justified by faith, then you can rejoice in the hope of the glory of God. You may be in difficult circumstances, and you may hurt. Your body may be in pain. But you can still rejoice because, as a Christian, you have peace with God, you have access to God, you are standing in grace, and you have hope. You can rejoice in that hope, because one day you are going to share in the glory of God!

RELATIONSHIP TO CIRCUMSTANCES

A second mark of justification is our new relationship to circumstances (Rom. 5:3–4). The unsaved person is torn down by tribulations, but the believer is built up by tribulations. "Not only so, but we also rejoice in our sufferings" (v. 3). That doesn't mean we go out and look for them, but when trials do come, we don't give up, because we know that "suffering produces perseverance." The word *perseverance* doesn't mean sitting there stoically, just passively enduring suffering. It means brave endurance that keeps you going. It is not someone sitting in a rocking chair; it is the soldier out on the battlefield who keeps on going when the going gets tough. When you have been justified, when you are right with God, you are not bowled over by circumstances.

What life does to you depends upon what life finds in you. If you have peace with God within, if you have the grace of God, if you are rejoicing in the hope of the glory of God, then suffering is going to work for you and not against you. Suffering works "brave endurance," and endurance works "tested character." When you know God, nothing builds character like trials.

Circumstances by themselves do not build character. I have seen circumstances tear people down. But when you know God, circumstances can build character. The word *tribulation* comes from a Latin word, *tribulum*. A *tribulum* was a huge piece of wood (like a railroad tie) that had nails driven into it, and the oxen used to draw this piece of wood over the threshing floor to thresh the grain. This is what suffering can do for us. Tribulation is God's way of separating the wheat from the chaff, the grain from the waste. And tribulation works *for* us because it develops brave endurance in us. When you have brave endurance, you start building character, and character produces hope. The most hopeful Christians I have met have been those who have gone through the threshing of tribulation.

When you have been justified by faith, you have a right relationship with God, and you have a right relationship to the circumstances around you. Circumstances are not tearing you down; they are building you up.

RELATIONSHIP TO OTHERS

Third, you have a right relationship to others. "And hope does not disappoint us, because God has poured out his love into our hearts by the Holy Spirit, whom he has given us" (Rom. 5:5). This is a part of "justification that brings life" that is mentioned in verse 18. When you are justified by faith, when you trust the Savior, the Holy Spirit comes into your life and you know that you are one of God's children. The Holy Spirit gives to you the fullness of God's love. "And hope does not disappoint us, because God has poured out his love into our hearts through the Holy Spirit" (Rom. 5:5). This means you allow love to rule in your relationships.

When you have this kind of love in your heart, it isn't hard to get along with other people, even difficult people. We have all experienced the change that took place because we trusted the Savior. We replaced hatred, jealousy, envy, and selfishness with love. The Holy Spirit began to produce in our lives the fruit of the Spirit listed here: Love in verse 5, hope in verse 2, peace in verse 1. The love of God, the peace of God, and the hope that we have in God are all the result of justification by faith.

It is a marvelous thing to be justified! There is no reason in all the world why we Christians should be walking around with long faces, with dismal expressions, always complaining. We have so much, because we have trusted Christ as our Savior! If you have been justified, you have a right relationship with God; you have peace with God, not war; you have access to God; you have grace from God, and you can get through life with all of His power; and you can rejoice in the hope of the glory of God.

More than that, you have a right relationship to circumstances. The difficult circumstances of life will not tear you down; they will build you up. They will build character and brave endurance, and they will give you a blessed hope. You will have a right relationship to others. The love of God in your heart will flow out through your life, and you will find yourself getting along with people and glorifying God. These are the marks of justification.

Have you received Christ as your Savior? Can you say, "Being justified by faith, I have peace with God"?

4

Adoption into the Family of God

Since I was the last of four children, I knew very little about seniority rights. Those of you who have older brothers or sisters know what I am talking about. When I was born again into God's family, I was happy to discover that in His family there are no seniority rights. Instead, God has given to every one of His children a wonderful experience known as adoption. An understanding of adoption is important if you and I are to enjoy our Christian life to the fullest. To help us understand this doctrine, I'm going to answer three questions: What is adoption? What are the privileges of adoption? How can we enjoy adoption?

WHAT IS ADOPTION?

Adoption is the act of God by which He gives each of His children an adult standing in His family. Adoption is not the way you get into God's family. The only way to get into God's family is by regeneration, being born again. When a couple adopts a child, it is a beautiful experience. They can give that child their name, their address, their home, their wealth; but they cannot give that adopted child their nature. That child will always have the nature of his or her parents. The only way to get into God's family is to have God's nature and share God's life, and that can come only by regeneration.

Adoption is not the way you get into God's family; adoption is the way you _enjoy_ God's family. Adoption is the act of God by which He gives each of His children an adult standing in His family. The instant you were saved you received an adult standing, which means you have all the adult privileges. You also have adult responsibilities.

This means that you and I cannot use the length of time we have been saved as an excuse for being poor Christians. Someone may say, "Well, I have only been saved for four or five years; you can't expect too much of me." God says, "No, I expect of you what I expect of every one of My children. I am going to give you adult privileges, and I expect from you adult conduct and the fulfillment of adult responsibilities." That is what adoption is. Adoption means that the instant you were born into His family, God gave you an adult standing.

WHAT ARE THE PRIVILEGES OF ADOPTION?

Many of the privileges of adoption are listed in Romans 8:14–17:

Those who are led by the Spirit of God are sons of God. For you did not receive a spirit that makes you a slave again to fear, but you received the Spirit of sonship. And by him we cry, "Abba, Father." The Spirit himself testifies with our spirit that we are God's children. Now if we are children, then we are heirs—heirs of God and co-heirs with Christ, if indeed we share in his sufferings in order that we may also share in his glory.

We have listed here at least six privileges of adoption. I wonder how many of these privileges you and I have been claiming?

Walking

First, there is the privilege of walking. "Because those who are led by the Spirit of God are sons of God" (Rom. 8:14). That verb *led* means "willingly led." You can't lead a little baby, because a baby cannot walk. A baby has to be carried. But when you enter God's family, you are adopted, and instantly you are able to walk.

The unsaved person walks according to the course of this world; he walks according to the ruler of the kingdom of the air; he walks in disobedience (see Eph. 2:2). But you and I have the privilege of walking in obedience, because we are led by the Spirit of God. God has a plan for our lives; He has a path on which we should walk. Romans 6:4 tells us we walk in newness of life. Romans 8:4 tells us that we walk not after the flesh but after the Spirit. We have the freedom and the blessing and the privilege of walking.

Freedom

That leads to our second privilege—the privilege of freedom. "For you did not receive a spirit that makes you a slave again to fear, but you received the Spirit of son-ship" (Rom. 8:15). Under the Law there was bondage. The Jewish nation had to obey, and if they did not obey, they would be judged.

Consider Galatians 4:1–7:

> What I am saying is that as long as the heir is a child, he is no different from a slave, although he owns the whole estate. He is subject to guardians and trustees until the time set by his father. So also, when we were children, we were in slavery under the basic principles of the world. But when the time had fully come, God sent his Son, born of a woman, born under law, to redeem those under law, that we might receive the full rights of sons. Because you are sons, God sent the Spirit of his Son into our hearts, the Spirit who calls out, "Abba, Father." So you are no longer a slave, but a son; and since you are a son, God has made you also an heir.

There is a contrast here between being a servant and being a son. The word *son* refers to a mature son, not just a little baby. When you are a child, you are under all kinds of rules and regulations. "Don't do this, and don't do that. Don't touch this, and don't go there." Sad to say, many Christians live like this; they live a life of legalistic bondage. Paul informs us that the Holy Spirit who has come into our lives is the Spirit of adoption. We have not received "a spirit that makes you a slave again to fear" (Rom. 8:15). I suppose these two words best describe little children—*fear* and *bondage*. They are always afraid of something, and they are in bondage—they must always obey others. They are under the control of parents and teachers. You and I, as God's adopted children, have freedom from the Law. This does not mean we are lawless; it does mean that our relationship to our Father is one of love and not of bondage. We have freedom; we are able to walk.

Speaking *Prayings*

Third, we have the privilege of speaking. Romans 8:15 states that we receive the Spirit of adoption, "and by him we cry, 'Abba, Father.'" According to Galatians 4, when the Holy Spirit comes into our hearts, He cries, "Abba, Father," and then *we* are able to cry, "Abba, Father." (Abba is the Hebrew word for "papa" or "daddy.") No baby is born speaking. That would be a remarkable thing if a child could instantly speak. But when you were born into God's family, even though you were only one second old in the Lord, you were adopted and had the privilege of speaking—speaking *to* God in prayer, in praise, and in worship and speaking *for* God in witness.

Assurance

The fourth privilege is found in Romans 8:16—the privilege of assurance. We *know* we are God's children. Notice what it says: "The Spirit himself testifies with our spirit that we are God's children." No little baby knows it is a baby. It doesn't even know it is a human being. It has to grow into this knowledge. No baby knows who his parents are. A baby gets to know very early that certain people are very close to him and are very meaningful to him, but he doesn't know how to call them Father or Mother. When you and I were born again and adopted, instantly we knew we were God's children. Instantly we knew who our Father was and were able to look up and say, "Abba, Father." "Abba" expresses our close, intimate, loving relationship with our heavenly Father.

Inheritance

We have a fifth privilege—the privilege of inheritance. Romans 8:17 says, "Now if we are children, then we are heirs—heirs of God and co-heirs with Christ." No baby can inherit anything. If the parents die, and they leave their estate to their baby, that baby has to be under trustees until he or she can legally inherit the wealth. You and I do not have to wait to mature to inherit our wealth. If that were the case, we would never grow up. We need that spiritual wealth now in order to mature in Christ.

In Romans 8:17 we are told that we are now the heirs of God and joint-heirs with Christ. That means everything we inherit comes through Christ. There are two names on the check: Our Lord Jesus signs the check, and we have to sign the check. This is what prayer is all about. This is why we come "in the name of Jesus," because apart from Him we can inherit nothing.

As a Christian, you are rich today. Ishmael was Abraham's firstborn son, born of Hagar, but Ishmael was born poor. Isaac was born rich. You and I were born rich in Jesus Christ. We have the riches of His grace, the riches of His wisdom, and the riches of His mercy. We can draw upon all of His riches in glory by Christ Jesus.

Suffering

Finally, we have the privilege of suffering. Romans 8:17 says that "we share in his sufferings in order that we may also share in his glory." We do everything we can to shield babies from suffering. If a baby starts to suffer, we drop everything to make that baby comfortable. But God allows His children to suffer because we aren't babies. He is treating us as adults.

We need suffering because it builds character. We need suffering because it builds spiritual muscles. Suffering teaches us much about the grace of God, and suffering prepares us for future glory. "We share in his sufferings in order that we may also share in his glory" (Rom. 8:17). God gives us the privilege of suffering because He wants us to grow up. The ultimate privilege of life is to be entrusted with God's glory. God puts us through suffering that He might be able to share His glory with us. That is an amazing thing!

Are you living up to your privileges? If you are a Christian, you have been adopted, you have an adult standing in the family of God. With this standing comes responsibility. We don't run away from suffering. We don't waste our inheritance. We are sure that we are born again, and we share this with others. We have the privilege of speaking to and for God and the freedom of walking with God. What privileges we have!

How Can We Enjoy Adoption?

Believe

To begin with, we can enjoy adoption by believing that it is true. Adoption is not a feeling; it is a fact. Just believe that it is true. Look at yourself in the mirror and say, "You are being treated as an adult, not as a little baby." God does not pamper His children. He will have no pampered children at all, because pampered children cannot be used for His glory. So just believe it and say, "Thank God I have been adopted; I have an adult standing before God. All these privileges are mine."

Yield

Second, yield to the Holy Spirit, for He is the Spirit of adoption. He is the one who will make all of this real to you. In Romans 8:2, He is called the Spirit of life. In Romans 8:13, we see He is the Spirit of death—He puts to death the deeds of the body. Yield to the Holy Spirit and claim God's promise by faith. The blessing is there; it is true, and it is real. Start treating yourself the way God treats you. Look upon yourself as an adult son or daughter in His family. Stop pampering yourself. Stop whimpering. Stop asking God to give you toys; ask Him to give you tools and weapons, because there is a Church to build and a battle to fight. It is a marvelous thing to be adopted and to be rich in the Lord Jesus Christ.

Regeneration

THE NEW BIRTH

THE WORD *regeneration* simply means new birth, renewal, or restoration. It is used only twice in our Authorized Version of the Bible. In Titus 3:5, we read about a personal regeneration: "Not because of righteous things we had done, but because of his mercy. He saved us through the washing of rebirth and renewal by the Holy Spirit." Do not allow that word *washing* to make you think of baptism, because regeneration—being born again—does not come through baptism. The word *washing* in Titus 3:5 is parallel to the word *renewal* at the end of the verse: "the washing of rebirth and renewal by the Holy Spirit." Personal regeneration, or rebirth, is the work of the Holy

Spirit in the life of the person who trusts Christ as his Savior.

There is also a universal regeneration. Our Lord speaks about this in Matthew 19:28: "Jesus said to them, 'I tell you the truth, at the renewal [regeneration] of all things, when the Son of Man sits on his glorious throne, you who have followed me will also sit on twelve thrones, judging the twelve tribes of Israel.'" Our Lord tells us there is going to be a future regeneration of this world when He will sit upon a throne and He will judge and there will be glory and perfection.

The word *regeneration* simply means the act of God by which new life is imparted to the person who trusts Christ as his Savior. Justification gives me a righteous standing before God and adoption gives me an adult standing before God, but regeneration, or rebirth, gives me the life of God, the nature of God, in my very being.

Regeneration does not simply put us back to where we would have been had Adam never sinned. Regeneration is birth into a brand-new life; it is sharing the very life of God. It is not just a reformation. If regeneration were only reformation, you would lose it the next time you sinned. No, regeneration is that act of God whereby the very life of God is communicated to those who trust Christ as their Savior.

The classic text on regeneration is John 3:

Now there was a man of the Pharisees named Nicodemus, a member of the Jewish ruling council. He came to Jesus at night and said, "Rabbi, we know you are a teacher who has come from God. For no one could perform the miraculous signs you are doing if God were not with him."

In reply Jesus declared, "I tell you the truth, no one can see the kingdom of God unless he is born again."

"How can a man be born when he is old?" Nicodemus asked. "Surely he cannot enter a second time into his mother's womb to be born!"

Jesus answered, "I tell you the truth, no one can enter the kingdom of God unless he is born of water and the Spirit. Flesh gives birth to flesh, but the Spirit gives birth to spirit. You should not be surprised at my saying, 'You must be born again.' The wind blows wherever it pleases. You hear its sound, but you cannot tell where it comes from or where it is going. So it is with everyone born of the Spirit."

"How can this be?" Nicodemus asked.

VERSES 1–9

This passage has been preached upon and taught for many, many centuries. It is familiar to us. In fact, I trust its familiarity does not rob us of its true meaning. There are several facts about regeneration, the new birth, that need to be understood, and they are given to us in this passage.

REALITY OF THE NEW BIRTH

First of all, we are confronted with the reality of the new birth. The word *born* is used six times in John 3:1–9. Jesus was talking about a real experience—the reality of the new birth. There are those who tell us that this experience of regeneration is psychological, that people can even have this kind of experience apart from faith in Jesus Christ. There are false religions and psychological approaches to religion that tell us that the new birth happens because of some psychological experience. But the new birth is a reality; it is as real as physical birth.

No one would deny his own physical birth, and we do not have to deny our spiritual birth. Jesus said that the new birth is a reality. If you would interview people who trusted Jesus, you would find out how real it is. Ask Peter; he knew what it was to trust in Jesus Christ and to experience this new birth. In his letters, Peter tells us about this matter of being born again. Matthew, the publican, had his life radically changed because he trusted Christ and experienced the new birth. The thief on the cross turned to Jesus and said, "Remember me when you come into your kingdom" (Luke 23:42). Because of his faith in Christ, he was born again. Ask him whether or not rebirth is a real experience.

Ask the apostle Paul. Saul of Tarsus, the leading young Jewish rabbi of his day, was persecuting the church when he met Jesus Christ. He put his faith in Jesus, and he was born again. It was a real experience.

When our Lord was ministering here on earth, everybody had some answers to the problems of life. The Romans said the way to solve life's problems is through law, and you back up that law with the military. The Greeks said the way to solve problems is with wisdom. People need schools, understanding, and philosophy. Of course the Jewish people said the answer is religion. You need sacrifices, a priesthood, the temple. Jesus said the answer is in the heart. Law will never change the heart; wisdom will never change the heart; religion will never change the heart. But regeneration will. The reality of the new birth, the good news of the gospel, is this: You can start all over again! You do not have to stay the way you are. Because there is such a thing as regeneration, you can be born again.

SIMPLICITY OF THE NEW BIRTH

Next, we must understand the simplicity of the new birth. Our Lord Jesus used birth as a simple illustration of what happens when a person is saved. Even though he was a great teacher of Israel, Nicodemus unfortunately misunderstood what our Lord was talking about. "'How can a man be born when he is old?' Nicodemus asked. 'Surely he cannot enter a second time into his mother's womb to be born!'" (John 3:4). Our Lord was talking about something spiritual, but Nicodemus interpreted it as something physical.

In John 4, when our Lord was talking to the woman at the well, He talked about living water. He said, "If you knew the gift of God and who it is that asks you for a drink, you would have asked him and he would have given you living water. . . . but whoever drinks the water I give him will never thirst. Indeed, the water I give him will become in him a spring of water welling up to eternal life" (vv. 10, 14). He was speaking spiritually, but she took Him literally and materially: "You have nothing to draw with and the well is deep. Where can you get this living water?" (v. 11).

In John 6, our Lord was talking about eating the Bread of Life, feeding on Christ through the Word. The Jews were offended by this. But He wasn't speaking in material terms. He Himself tells us that it is the Spirit that gives life; the flesh profits nothing (see v. 63).

When Jesus spoke about birth, Nicodemus took Him literally. Jesus replied in John 3:5–6, "No one can enter the kingdom of God unless he is born of water and the Spirit. Flesh gives birth to flesh, but the Spirit gives birth to spirit." Our Lord was saying, "Nicodemus, please don't major on the physical and the material—I'm talking in spiritual terms."

Two parents create this new birth—the Spirit of God and the Word of God, according to James 1:18 and 1 Peter 1:23. We are born again by the living Word of God. The Spirit of God takes the Word of God and reveals the Son of God. And when you trust Jesus Christ as your Savior, a miracle takes place in your heart—regeneration; you are born again. The two "spiritual parents" who accomplish this birth are the Spirit of God and the Word of God.

The Bible makes it very clear in John 1:13 that we are not born of the flesh, we are not born of the will of man, and we are not born of our own efforts. No baby is conceived and born of his own effort. We are born by the Spirit of God.

Mystery is involved. In John 3:8 Christ says, "The wind blows wherever it pleases. You hear its sound, but you cannot tell where it comes from or where it is going. So it is with everyone born of the Spirit." He is not comparing the wind to the Holy Spirit, although that is a valid illustration. He is comparing the believer to the wind: "So it is with everyone born of the Spirit." There is mystery to physical birth; there is mystery to spiritual birth. But just think of how simple it is: Trust Jesus Christ and you will be born again.

DIGNITY OF THE NEW BIRTH

A third fact comes to our attention—the dignity of the new birth. The word translated "born again" can be translated "born from above." We are born children of the King, children of God. "Yet to all who received him, to those who believed in his name, he gave the right to become children of God" (John 1:12). "How great is the love the Father has lavished on us, that we should be called children of God!" (1 John 3:1). The dignity of the new birth is an amazing thing.

Children like to be proud of their parents. If we have a relative who is somebody important, we like to talk about it. We become name-droppers. You and I share the dignity of the new birth; we are the children of God—the God who created the universe, the God and Father of our Lord Jesus Christ. We are in His family; we share His nature. I have the nature of my parents, and my children have my nature. We have God's nature within because we have been born from above, and this new nature creates a new disposition.

When you are one of God's children and you share God's nature, you live the way God wants you to live. God is love, and so we love; God is light, and so we walk as children of light. We share His nature and His life, and people can see a difference in our lives.

URGENCY OF THE NEW BIRTH

Finally, we must come to realize the urgency of the new birth. Jesus said, "You must be born again" (John 3:7). It is not a suggestion; it is a commandment. It is not an idea that we can toy with; it is absolutely urgent—we must be born again. The new birth is instantaneous; it is not a process. There may be a process of preparation; you may have a desire to know God or a concern about getting rid of sin. But the birth itself is instantaneous, supernatural, and permanent.

Once you are born, you can't be unborn. You may be disobedient or you may not grow as you should, but you cannot be unborn. Our spiritual birth is a permanent, supernatural birth, and there is urgency to it. "No one can see the kingdom of God unless he is born again" (v. 3). The god of this world blinds those who do not believe. Until you are born again, you cannot see what you are missing; you cannot see what you really are; you cannot see all that God has for you. You must be born again not only to see the kingdom of God, but to *enter* the kingdom of God. "I tell you the truth, no one can enter the kingdom of God unless he is born of water and the Spirit" (v. 5).

When you were born the first time ("born of water"), you entered into the kingdom of sin and Satan. You lived according to the course of this world, and you followed the dictates of Satan. But when you entered the kingdom of God through regeneration, then you became a part of that kingdom, which is wonderful, eternal, and glorious. The only way to escape eternal judgment is through faith in Christ. "For God so loved the world that he gave his one and only Son, that whoever believes in him shall not perish but have eternal life" (v. 16).

Have you been thinking about this? Has God been talking to you? The reality of the new birth is that you can change; God will change you when you trust Christ. The simplicity of the new birth is that it is not through religion or good works, but through trust in the Savior. Imagine becoming a child of God and enjoying the dignity of the new birth! The urgency of the new birth is that you *must* be born again. If God has been talking to you about this, then open your heart now to Jesus Christ.

6

Propitiation

SATISFACTION OF GOD'S HOLINESS

PROPITIATION IS ONE of those technical words in the New Testament that we need to understand. "God presented him as a sacrifice of atonement [propitiation], through faith in his blood. He did this to demonstrate his justice, because in his forbearance he had left the sins committed beforehand unpunished" (Rom. 3:25).

When you walk into the Book of Romans, you walk into a court of law. There you and I stand before God, the Judge. We are guilty. We are criminals who are guilty of disobeying God's Law. Our standing before God has been forfeited. Not only are we criminals, we are prisoners— we are in bondage. Our condition is one of bondage and agony. I cannot conceive of a lost sinner enjoying life, for he has nothing to enjoy. The very sword of God's judgment hangs over his head. We are condemned; we face the wrath of God.

When we look *back,* we realize we are guilty of disobedience. When we look *around,* we realize we are prisoners. When we look *ahead,* we realize we are condemned; we have no future. The Book of Romans teaches this very clearly.

How can we get out of this terrible plight? We are helpless; we can't do it ourselves. The Judge may love us and want to help us all that he can, but he has to obey the Law. The only solution is that someone can come in, obey the Law, fulfill the righteous demands of the Law, and set us free. Of course, that person is Jesus Christ. This is what propitiation is all about.

DEFINITION OF PROPITIATION

Let us consider this wonderful doctrine from three different aspects. First of all, the definition of propitiation: Propitiation is the work of Jesus Christ on the cross by which He satisfied God's holiness so God could extend mercy to lost sinners. If you look up the word *propitiation* in an English dictionary, you will find it defined as "appeasing someone's anger." Some people think God the Father is angry at lost sinners. They think He is sitting in heaven waiting to throw thunderbolts upon people who have disobeyed Him. Then God the Son comes up and says, "Now, Father, please don't be angry! I will go and die for these sinners, and this will appease Your wrath." Nothing could be further from the truth.

To begin with, Jesus Christ and His Father and the Holy Spirit work together in this great plan of salvation. It is not that one wants to condemn and the other wants to forgive. When Jesus went to the cross of Calvary, the Father was there. It is true the Father forsook His Son when His Son was made sin, but that was just for a brief moment when our Savior cried out, "My God, my God, why have you forsaken me?" (Matt. 27:46). The Father and the Son and the Holy Spirit worked together in the plan of salvation. Propitiation does not mean that Jesus Christ came to appease God's anger because the Father doesn't love us.

Some people have the idea that, because of His death on the cross, our Lord turned God's wrath into love. Again, nothing could be further from the truth. Our God is a God of judgment. We want to be very clear about that. Throughout the Bible you find the revelation of the wrath of God as well as the mercy of God. There are almost twenty Hebrew words in the Old Testament translated "wrath." There are more than five hundred references to wrath and judgment just in the Old Testament. Our Father in heaven is a loving Father, but He is also a holy Father. He is love (see 1 John 4:8), but He is also light (see 1:5). God's anger does not turn into love, because this would mean that God is changing, and God does not change. Propitiation does not mean appeasing God's unloving anger; propitiation does not mean turning God's wrath into love. His wrath is a holy wrath; His judgment is a holy judgment. Because He loves holiness and hates sin, He has to be a God of judgment.

Propitiation means that Christ satisfied the holiness of God so that God is able to extend grace and mercy to lost sinners. God is a free God, and because He is holy, sin has to be punished. God cannot break His own Law. If for one instant God broke His Law, the universe would fall apart. All of God's attributes are consistent. His wisdom does not fight against His power. His power does not fight against His grace. His grace does not fight against His holiness. There is a cooperation, a consistency, a unity about the character of God.

You and I are not consistent. At times we are overly sentimental and loving; at other times we are overly angry and unforgiving. God is not this way. God's attributes are consistent and unified, and so there is no need for Him to lay one aside for the other. God's holiness demands that sin be punished. God cannot lie; God cannot break His own Law. His love moves Him to save the sinner, but His love is a *holy* love, and this is where propitiation comes in.

Jesus Christ satisfies the demands of the Law. Propitiation describes the God-ward work of Christ on the cross—He paid the penalty for the broken Law. The Law was satisfied. He lived a perfect life and bore the judgment of the guilty sinner on the cross, and sinners now can be justified. Forgiveness is now available because of God's grace. There is no condemnation, because Jesus Christ has died.

The old Puritan theologian John Owen summarized propitiation in four simple statements. First, there is an offense to be removed. Sinners have offended a holy God. Second, there is an offended person to be dealt with— God the Father. God the Father simply cannot close His eyes like some doting grandfather and say, "Well, I'll forget all about it." A holy God has to deal with sin. Third, the person who has offended has to be pardoned. If he is not pardoned, he is condemned. In order for this to happen, a sacrifice has to be offered. So there is an offense to be removed, an offended person to be satisfied, an offending person to be pardoned, and a sacrifice to be made to make this all possible. This is the meaning of propitiation.

DEMONSTRATION OF PROPITIATION

A demonstration of propitiation is found in Leviticus 16. You are acquainted, I'm sure, with the great Day of Atonement. Once a year the high priest laid aside his beautiful garments and offered sacrifices for his own sins. Then he set apart two goats: One goat was chosen to die, and the other goat was chosen to stay alive. The high priest would kill the goat that was set aside for sacrifice and take the blood of that goat into the Holy of Holies in the sanctuary of God. This was the only time in the year when the high priest was allowed to go into the Holy of Holies. He sprinkled the blood on the mercy seat, that beautiful golden covering on the ark of the covenant. At each end of the mercy seat there was a golden cherub, positioned as though looking down into the ark. In the ark were the tables of the Law. When the priest came in and sprinkled the blood upon that mercy seat, the blood covered the broken Law.

Then he would go out and put his hands on the head of the living goat and confess the sins of the people of Israel. That living goat was then taken out into the wilderness, turned loose, and never seen again. Together, these two goats made up a sin offering. It is a picture to us of John 1:29: "Look, the Lamb of God, who takes away the sin of the world!"

The Lord Jesus Christ died on the cross; His blood turned the throne of judgment into a throne of grace, a mercy seat. In fact, the word *propitiation* is translated "mercy seat" in Hebrews 9:5 (see NIV margin). God's justice has been satisfied, and now God can forgive our sins and take them from us as far as the east is from the west. The Law has been satisfied, and God is "free" to extend pardon and mercy. He can be just as He forgives our sins.

Dynamic of Propitiation

I want to close this chapter by talking about the dynamic of propitiation. If you know Jesus as your Savior, then you have all of the blessings that are wrapped up in propitiation. What are they?

Sinners Can Be Saved

First of all, sinners can be saved from judgment. We read in 1 John 4:10: "This is love: not that we loved God, but that he loved us and sent his Son as an atoning sacrifice for our sins." In 1 John 2:2 we read these words: "He is the atoning sacrifice for our sins, and not only for ours but also for the sins of the whole world." Propitiation says that sinners can be saved from judgment, and not just a few sinners—propitiation is available to the whole world.

When the Lord Jesus Christ rose from the dead and the tomb was left empty, Mary came to the tomb and stood outside weeping. When she stopped and looked in the tomb, she saw two angels—one at the head and one at the foot of where the body had been lying (see John 20:11–12). The garments our Lord had been wrapped in were lying there empty because He had risen from the dead. At each end of that stone slab there was an angel—it looked just like the mercy seat! Because Jesus died for us, sinners can be saved from judgment.

You are ready to give up. You are ready to quit. Sin has gotten such a hold on your life that you don't know what to do. I have good news for you: Christ is the propitiation for our sins, and not for ours only but for the sins of the whole world. This is a good motivation to get the gospel out to the whole world. Your church's ministry and your ministry ought to be one of worldwide missions as well as witnessing to people here at home. So the dynamic of propitiation is that sinners can be saved from judgment by trusting Jesus Christ.

Believers Can Be Forgiven

Second, believers can be forgiven when they sin. First John 2:1–2 says, "My dear children, I write this to you so that you will not sin. But if anybody does sin, we have one who speaks to the Father in our defense—Jesus Christ, the Righteous One. He is the atoning sacrifice for our sins, and not only for ours but also for the sins of the whole world." Because Jesus Christ died for our sins, He met the holy demands of God's just Law, and we can be forgiven. We don't have to be saved all over again; we are forgiven. We can come to the Lord Jesus Christ and confess our sins. He forgives us and restores us because we come to the mercy seat where His blood has been applied.

We Can Find Strength

There is a third dynamic to propitiation. It not only means forgiveness for lost sinners, a message for the whole world, and the assurance of forgiveness when we sin, but it means that we can find strength for living at the mercy seat. Hebrews 4:16 says, "Let us then approach the throne of grace with confidence, so that we may receive mercy and find grace to help us in our time of need." The mercy seat is the place where we meet God, where we meet Jesus Christ, and where we can find grace for the demands of life.

So the Lord Jesus Christ is our propitiation. He has provided all that is necessary for salvation, for daily forgiveness, for motivation to witness to the whole world, and for strength for daily living. I'm sure you have seen the name William Cowper in your hymnal at church. He was a discouraged man, a very nervous fellow, ready to give up. And he said in one of his writings, on a day when he was extremely distraught,

> I flung myself into a chair near the window, and seeing a Bible there, ventured once more to apply to it for comfort and instruction. The first verse I saw was the 25th of the 3rd of Romans: "Whom God hath set forth to be a

propitiation through faith in his blood." I saw the sufficiency of the atonement He had made, my pardon sealed in His blood, and all the fulness and completeness of His justification. In an instant I believed and received the peace of the gospel.

He wrote these words:

> There is a fountain filled with blood
> Drawn from Immanuel's veins,
> And sinners plunged beneath that flood
> Lose all their guilty stains.

Imputation

GOD CREDITS OUR ACCOUNT

SO IMPORTANT IS eternal life that the Bible gives us many illustrations so that no one will miss the message. To farmers, Jesus talked about soil and seed. To shepherds, He talked about sheep. To beggars, He talked about a great feast that God had spread. To lawyers, He talked about justification. To housewives, He talked about a coin that had been lost and had to be found. But when you use the word *imputation,* you find God speaking to the banker, because this is a financial term.

Romans 4:1–8 says,

> What then shall we say that Abraham, our forefather, discovered in this matter? If, in fact, Abraham was justified by works, he had something to boast about—but not before God. What does the Scripture say? "Abraham believed God, and it was credited to him [imputed] as righteousness."

Now when a man works, his wages are not credited to him [imputed] as a gift, but as an obligation. However, to the man who does not work but trusts God who justifies the wicked, his faith is credited [imputed] as righteousness. David says the same thing when he speaks of the blessedness of the man to whom God credits righteousness apart from works:

> "Blessed are they
> whose transgressions are forgiven,
> whose sins are covered.
> Blessed is the man
> whose sin the Lord will never count against him."

Our English word *imputation* comes from the Latin word that means "to reckon, or credit, to one's account." When you go to the bank or the savings and loan association and deposit money, imputation takes place. They deposit the money in your account, and they write it on your record.

We want to study imputation from three different aspects: first by way of explanation, then by way of example, and finally by way of experience.

EXPLANATION OF IMPUTATION

The easiest way to understand imputation is simply to see two record books, two bankbooks. One of them has Christ's name on it, and the other has Adam's name on it. The record book for our Lord Jesus Christ is perfect—there is no indebtedness whatsoever. He is absolutely righteous, and His record is spotless. The record book for Adam is imperfect—he is bankrupt! He has sinned and come short of the glory of God.

Our record is Adam's record because we are the children of Adam. Genesis 5:1 says, "This is the written account of Adam's line." The entire Old Testament is "the written account of Adam's line," and everyone named in the record is a failure. Then you turn to Matthew 1:1 and read: "The record of the genealogy of Jesus Christ." God opens a new record, and that record is perfect, because His Son's name is on it.

What can you and I do about this imperfect record that is on our account? As far as God's "spiritual bank" is concerned, we are bankrupt—we fall short. God has audited the books and discovered that you and I do not have anything with which to pay our debt. What shall we do about it?

Well, we could ignore it, and most people do. Most people don't think about their debt to God. They have broken His Law; they have gone beyond His barriers. He has said, "This far and no farther," and they have said, "We're going to do it anyway." Then they try to ignore their disobedience. But a day of reckoning is coming, and that day may be soon.

A man can work for a bank and secretly be stealing money and falsifying the records, but eventually a day of reckoning comes, and he is caught. We can ignore it, but the day of reckoning is going to come.

We could try to change the record ourselves, but we are too bankrupt to do this. We simply do not have the spiritual capital necessary to wipe out our spiritual debt to God. Can we destroy the book? No, that book is in God's hands; no one can destroy that record. How, then, can we solve the problem of our spiritual bankruptcy, the debt that we have to God? Well, the answer is imputation, and Jesus Christ is the one who comes with the solution. What did He do?

Christ Took Our Debt

First of all, He took our debt. That is a remarkable thing. When our Lord Jesus Christ came to earth, He came to die.

God made Christ, who knew no sin, to be sin for us. Why? "That in him we might become the righteousness of God" (2 Cor. 5:21). In Isaiah 53:12 we are told that He was reckoned among the transgressors. That word *reckon* means "counted." In other words, He was counted as a transgressor. He was made poor that we might become rich (see 2 Cor. 8:9). He took our debt.

He Gave Us His Righteousness

But that leaves me with a problem: If He takes my debt, then the next time I sin I go back into debt again. So He did something else. He not only took our debt, but He credited His own righteousness to our account. Romans 4:6 says, "David says the same thing when he speaks of the blessedness of the man to whom God credits righteousness apart from works." *Imputation* means "putting it to our account."

You must not confuse imputation with impartation. Let me explain. Justification means God puts His righteousness on our account. This is righteousness *imputed*. Right in the middle of that word *impute* you have *put*—righteousness put to our account. But sanctification is righteousness *imparted*—God shares His righteousness in our lives and enables us to live a holy life. So Jesus Christ paid our debt; He assumed our bankruptcy. Second, He credited His righteousness to our account so that we have the righteousness of Christ on our record. That is a remarkable thing.

But once again, I ask the question, What about the next time I sin? Romans 4:8 says, "Blessed is the man whose sin the Lord will never count against him." Once the righteousness of Christ has been put on our record, how could God ever record sin? Can He record our sin along with the righteousness of Christ? Of course not. The righteousness of Jesus Christ is written on our record. "Blessed are they whose transgressions are forgiven, whose sins are covered. Blessed is the man whose sin the Lord will never count against him" (vv. 7–8). So there is the negative—He took our debt—and the positive—He credits His righteousness to our account. He does not record our sin.

EXAMPLE OF IMPUTATION

Now let's look at imputation by way of example. The most beautiful example of imputation is found in a letter that Paul wrote to his friend Philemon. I think you probably know the story. Philemon had a slave named Onesimus. Onesimus stole something from his master, Philemon, and fled to the city of Rome, trying to hide. In the providence of God, Onesimus met Paul and was converted. Paul wrote this letter to Philemon on behalf of Onesimus, because he wanted Philemon to forgive Onesimus and restore him.

Onesimus is a picture of the lost sinner. He was a slave. He had no freedom of his own; he was in bondage. He was a thief; he had robbed his master. A slave was not treated with much kindness and mercy in those days. Onesimus deserved to die. He tried to run away. He was a lawbreaker, and he was caught. And yet Paul loved him, and God loved him, so Paul wrote these words to Philemon in verse 18: "If he has done you any wrong or owes you anything, charge it to me." Isn't that thrilling? Paul was saying, "I want you to impute his debt to me. He stole from you, and he has probably sold what he had stolen and spent the money. He is broke and he is bankrupt, but you put that on my account." That is imputation.

But that is not enough. Verse 17 says, "So if you consider me a partner, welcome him as you would welcome me." That is the positive part. He said, "When Onesimus comes home, don't see Onesimus; see Paul. Receive him the way you would receive me."

The Lord Jesus Christ did that for us. He said to God the Father, "Warren Wiersbe is bankrupt. He couldn't begin to pay his debt. Put it on My account." He died for me, and now He says to God the Father, "Whenever you see Warren Wiersbe, see Your own Son. Receive him as You would receive Me." That is imputation. It is marvelous, isn't it, that God should not only pay our debt, but that He should give us His righteousness? Then He says, "Your sins and your iniquities will I remember no more. I am no longer keeping a record."

God does keep a record of our works, and of course our sins affect our works. We must not think that because God is not keeping a record of our sins, we can freely go out and sin. Of course, no born-again Christian wants to deliberately, habitually sin. In fact, people who live like that give evidence they have never really been born again. But this doctrine of imputation encourages us to seek cleansing when we do sin.

EXPERIENCE OF IMPUTATION

Now let's look at imputation by way of experience. How can we make this work in our lives?

Admit Your Debt

First of all, admit your debt. If you have never been born again, if you have never been saved, just admit that you are in debt, that you are bankrupt, and that you can't pay it yourself.

You will remember that in Luke 7:36–50, Jesus had a meeting with Simon the Pharisee. While He was having dinner with the Pharisee, a woman of the streets came in and wept and washed our Lord's feet, and the Pharisee was offended. Jesus told a story about two people who were in debt. In modern language, one owed a thousand dollars and one owed ten dollars. But the man to whom they owed this debt freely forgave them both. Now Jesus said to this Pharisee, "Which one of those two people is going to love him the most?" The Pharisee said, "Well, I suppose the one who had the most forgiven." But he didn't realize that he himself was in debt. He said, "Oh, this woman of the streets, she is in debt to God. She has broken God's Law. But Simon the Pharisee hasn't." Jesus said, "Now, wait a minute. You are just as much in debt as she is and maybe more because you don't see it the way she does. Furthermore, you are just as bankrupt." Admit your debt and receive by grace God's gift of righteousness.

Don't Record Your Own Sins

Second, don't keep books on yourself. Some Christians are always remembering what God has forgotten and forgetting what God wants them to remember. It is good for us to say, "Search me, O God, and know my heart" (Ps. 139:23). But it is also good for us not to keep a record of our sins. God is not keeping a record of our sins, so why should we? The devil loves to have us do this. Satan enjoys it when God's people wallow around in self-pity, remembering their past sins, and get discouraged and feel guilty. God has forgiven; God has put His righteousness on your book, and He is not keeping a record of your sins.

Don't Record Others' Sins

Third, don't keep a record of other people's sins. First Corinthians 13:5 reminds us that love does not keep a record of wrongs. Don't keep in your mind and heart a record of the bad things people have done to you. Just turn it over to God. God is not keeping a record; why should you? Just lovingly forgive them.

God Records Our Works

Finally, remember that God is keeping a record of our works. He has given us righteousness that we might live righteous lives. Righteousness is not only *imputed* (put on our account), but through the Holy Spirit righteousness is *imparted*. Let's be faithful. Let's rejoice at this wonderful freedom that we have. We do not have this debt hanging over our head. We have been forgiven. We have a record that is clean. The righteousness of Jesus Christ has been put to our account.

It is no wonder that David said, "Blessed is he whose transgressions are forgiven, whose sins are covered. Blessed is the man whose sin the Lord does not count against him and in whose spirit is no deceit" (Ps. 32:1–2). God has written His righteousness on your record; now let Him write that righteousness on your life.

Sanctification

HOLINESS AND OBEDIENCE

SANCTIFICATION IS the gracious work of God in setting the believer apart for Himself and for service in the world. Sanctification has three aspects to it. The theologians call them positional sanctification, practical, or progressive, sanctification, and perfect sanctification.

POSITIONAL SANCTIFICATION

Positional sanctification means that, in Christ, we have been set apart to belong to God and to serve Him. Positional sanctification never changes. First Corinthians 1:2 says, "To the church of God in Corinth, to those sanctified in Christ Jesus and called to be holy, together with all those everywhere who call on the name of our Lord Jesus Christ—their Lord and ours."

You can hardly call the people in the church at Corinth godly people. Some of them were getting drunk; some of them were living in immorality; some of them were suing each other. And yet Paul addressed them as a church (called-out people), sanctified in Christ Jesus. That is positional sanctification; it never changes.

PRACTICAL, OR PROGRESSIVE, SANCTIFICATION

Practical, or progressive, sanctification has to do with our everyday life. Our Lord Jesus prayed, "Sanctify them by the truth; your word is truth" (John 17:17). Since we have a holy position in Christ, we should live like it.

One theologian said, "It is one thing for sin to live in us; another for us to live in sin." We can't help the fact that our old nature is a sinful nature. But God has given us a new nature, and this new nature enables us to live a holy life. This is practical, or progressive, sanctification—day by day becoming more like the Savior, day by day overcoming sin and temptation, day by day growing stronger in spiritual things.

I want to focus on 2 Corinthians 7:1: "Since we have these promises, dear friends, let us purify ourselves from everything that contaminates body and spirit, perfecting holiness out of reverence for God." In this verse we have a series of dual truths. If we understand these truths, it will help us in our progressive sanctification.

Two Aspects of Sin

To begin with, Paul pointed out that there are two different aspects to sin: There are sins of the flesh, and there are sins of the spirit. "Let us purify ourselves from everything that contaminates body and spirit" (2 Cor. 7:1). In other words, we have here the prodigal son (he was guilty of sins of the flesh) and the elder brother (he was guilty of sins of the spirit). When David committed adultery with Bathsheba, that was a sin of the flesh. When David numbered the people in pride and rebelled against God, that was a sin of the spirit. There are sins of action, and there are sins of attitude.

Sins of the Flesh

Let's talk about these sins of the flesh. By the flesh, of course, Paul meant the old nature. When you and I were born again, God gave us a new nature, but He did not change the old nature. You and I are capable of sinning today. We don't *want* to, because the desires of the new nature have lifted us higher. But now we see what sin is really like. The Word of God and the Spirit of God have revealed to us the awfulness of sin, and we want nothing to do with it. But we are capable of sinning.

Everything the Bible has to say about the flesh is negative. "The Spirit gives life; the flesh counts for nothing" (John 6:63). We are to have no confidence in the flesh (see Phil. 3:3). The flesh is that which produces sin. Out of the heart of man (the old nature) comes all sorts of evil things—lying and lust and all the things that wreck our lives and ruin our testimonies. Galatians 5:19–21 has recorded the works of the flesh, and seventeen different sins are mentioned there. In Romans 1:19–32, at least twenty-four different sins are mentioned. The flesh is very productive when it comes to producing sin, and the flesh cannot be changed. We need to cleanse ourselves from all filthiness of the flesh.

Sins of the Spirit

There are also sins of the spirit. You and I may not be guilty of drunkenness, adultery, gluttony, or laziness, but how about pride, stubbornness, or criticism? G. Campbell Morgan used to call the sins of the spirit "sins in good standing." You have to be careful about them. You may not be a prodigal son, but you might be an elder brother—so critical that you won't fellowship with your brother. There are two aspects of sin, and we have to deal with them both—the filthiness of the flesh and also the filthiness of the spirit.

Two Aspects of Holiness

Second Corinthians 7:1 reveals that there are also two aspects to holiness. There is a negative aspect—"let us purify ourselves"—and a positive aspect—"perfecting holiness out of reverence for God."

Cleansing

"Let us purify ourselves" means *once and for all* let us cleanse out of our lives the defilement of sin. In fact, Paul wrote about this in 2 Corinthians 6:14–18. "Do not be yoked together with unbelievers" (v. 14). This is a farm picture. You don't yoke an ox and an ass together. They have two different temperaments, and they are not going to be able to work together. Believers should not be yoked together with unbelievers in marriage or in business.

"For what do righteousness and wickedness have in common?" (v. 14). The word *common* is a commercial term—it means "partnership." Righteousness cannot be in partnership with unrighteousness. "For what fellowship can light have with darkness?" (v. 14). The word *communion* means "to have in common." It is a family term. We do not have anything in common with unsaved people other than our humanity, because we are light and they are darkness. We have righteousness and they have unrighteousness.

"What harmony is there between Christ and Belial?" (v. 15). The word *harmony* here is a musical term. We aren't even playing in the same orchestra with the unsaved! We aren't following the same conductor or reading the same score. Therefore, how can we ever make music together? It is such a sad thing when believers try to manufacture harmony with unbelievers. You can't make a beautiful home that way.

"What does a believer have in common with an unbeliever? What agreement is there between the temple of God and idols? For we are the temple of the living God. As God has said: 'I will live with them and walk among them, and I will be their God, and they will be my people'" (vv. 15–16).

So the first aspect of holiness is to cleanse ourselves. This doesn't mean we become isolationists. We must live *in* the world but not *like* the world. We are to be the salt of the earth and the light of the world; we must have contact but not contamination. This is what the Bible calls separation—setting ourselves apart and saying, "I am not going to be yoked with unbelievers. I don't agree with them. I am not going to try to make music with unbelievers, because I just don't have the same conductor that they have." Separation—not isolation or insulation, but biblical separation—means cleansing ourselves.

Often we pray, "O God, cleanse me." And God comes back and says, "Why don't you cleanse yourself? Get rid of those videos. Get those books and magazines out of your library. Put away these things and be separate." Isaiah 1:16 says, "Wash and make yourselves clean."

Living in His Presence

It isn't enough to be negative like the Pharisees and *not* do certain things. We have to be positive, "perfecting holiness out of reverence for God" (2 Cor. 7:1). We have here a consistent, constant process. Holiness is what God is, and as we grow in holiness, we become more like God.

In the Old Testament tabernacle, there was a laver. The laver made cleansing possible. That's negative. But there was also a Holy of Holies. The priest was only allowed to enter there once a year. You and I can enter into God's presence at any time. In fact, we should *live* in His presence. The laver cleanses us, but being in fellowship with God in the Holy of Holies perfects us. Don't be afraid of holiness. Holiness is not the "brittle piety" that some people manifest—a religiosity that is artificial. No, holiness is *wholeness*. Holiness is to your soul what health is to your body. There are two aspects to sin—sins of the flesh and sins of the spirit. And there are two aspects to holiness—cleansing ourselves and perfecting holiness.

Two Aspects of Obedience

Finally, 2 Corinthians 7:1 reveals two motivations for obedience—love of God and fear of God.

Love of God

Why should we cleanse ourselves? Why should we perfect holiness? Because of God's love. "Since we have these promises, dear friends" (2 Cor. 7:1). What promises? "'Therefore come out from them and be separate,' says the Lord. 'Touch no unclean thing, and I will receive you. I will be a Father to you, and you will be my sons and daughters, says the Lord Almighty'" (6:17–18). Notice the promises here.

When you were saved, God became your Father. But He cannot be a Father to you if you are disobedient. We parents long to love our children and share the very best with them, but sometimes they won't let us. So God promises to receive us into a deeper fellowship if we are obedient. He will be a Father to us, and we will be His sons and daughters. Not only is His love available to us, but His power is also available to us, for He is the Lord Almighty. He promises to receive us. He promises to bless us. He promises a deeper fellowship with Him through the Word of God and through the Holy Spirit.

Listen to John 14:21–23:

> "Whoever has my commands and obeys them, he is the one who loves me. He who loves me will be loved by my Father, and I too will love him and show myself to him."
> Then Judas (not Judas Iscariot) said, "But, Lord, why do you intend to show yourself to us and not to the world?"
> Jesus replied, "If anyone loves me, he will obey my teaching. My Father will love him, and we will come to him and make our home with him."

That is a deeper fellowship with God, because we are cleansing ourselves and perfecting holiness in the fear of God.

Fear of God

The first motive for obedience is reverence; the second is fear—"perfecting holiness out of reverence for God" (2 Cor. 7:1). We don't have just God's promises; we also have God's discipline. If we do not walk in separation, God has to discipline us. He does not want us to become prisoners; He wants us to be sons and daughters who walk with Him. He says, "Therefore come out from them and be separate. . . . Touch no unclean thing, and I will receive you" (6:17). We do this out of reverence for God.

There is a sweet, deep fellowship with God that is so precious. There is also a walk with God that demands fear and reverence. We ought to reverence our Father in heaven, because it is He who has commanded us to be holy. This is practical, progressive sanctification—being aware of the sins of the flesh and of the spirit, being diligent to cleanse ourselves. We are motivated by the love of God because of His promises and by the fear of God because of His discipline. "Since we have these promises, dear friends, let us purify ourselves from everything that contaminates body and spirit, perfecting holiness out of reverence for God" (7:1).

PERFECT SANCTIFICATION

Perfect sanctification, of course, will take place when we see the Lord Jesus Christ at His coming, and we will be like Him, "for we shall see him as he is" (1 John 3:2).

These three aspects of sanctification relate to each other. Because we know we have been set apart by God and because we know that Jesus is coming and we will be like Him, we want to keep our lives clean today. We want to seek to become more like the Lord Jesus Christ.

Reconciliation

"Bring Us Together"

DURING THE 1968 presidential campaign, the town of Deshler, Ohio, became famous. One of the candidates was making a whistle-stop there. A thirteen-year-old girl picked up a sign that someone had dropped and held it up. The sign said, "Bring us together again." The news media coverage made the girl in Deshler, Ohio, famous overnight.

"Bring us together again." That's the cry of hearts today. There is a need for reconciliation, for people to be brought back together.

The Bible begins with a record of perfect harmony—heaven and earth working together in joyful cooperation. But then sin enters the picture, and you see division, dissention, death, and separation. Man is separated from God. Man runs from God and hides. And then man is separated from man, brother killing brother. There is a separation of races and nations as Genesis records the awful consequences of sin. The great need is for reconciliation, and that is the work of our Lord Jesus Christ.

Reconciliation means to bring together that which was separated or at war. Reconciliation involves the sinner, the Savior, and the believer.

THE SINNER

Reconciliation implies that the sinner is at war with God. Second Corinthians 5:17–21 says,

> Therefore, if anyone is in Christ, he is a new creation; the old has gone, the new has come! All this is from God, who reconciled us to himself through Christ and gave us the ministry of reconciliation: that God was reconciling the world to himself in Christ, not counting men's sins against them. And he has committed to us the message of reconciliation. We are therefore Christ's ambassadors, as though God were making his appeal through us. We implore you on Christ's behalf: Be reconciled to God. God made him who had no sin to be sin for us, so that in him we might become the righteousness of God.

Romans 5:7–10 says,

> Very rarely will anyone die for a righteous man, though for a good man someone might possibly dare to die. But God demonstrates his own love for us in this: While we were still sinners, Christ died for us. Since we have now been justified by his blood, how much more shall we be saved from God's wrath through him! For if, when we were God's enemies, we were reconciled to him through the death of his Son, how much more, having been reconciled, shall we be saved through his life!

Rome had two kinds of provinces—senatorial provinces and imperial provinces. What was the difference? The senatorial provinces were peaceful, and Rome did not put any troops there. The imperial provinces were the warlike provinces where there was trouble. Emperor Augustus ruled those provinces directly through his troops, and he always sent ambassadors to those provinces. The fact that God has chosen Christians to be His ambassadors in this world is an indication that the world is an "imperial province" at war with God.

Many people dispute this fact. They say that man is basically good. After all, not everybody is in jail, not everybody has broken the law. But the problem is, people look only on the surface; God sees the heart. Most people look only at actions and ignore motives. God sees the pride and rebellion in the human heart. The enmity between sinners and God is serious. If you have never been born again, then you are at war with God. "I know that nothing good lives in me" (Rom. 7:18). "The heart is deceitful above all things and beyond cure" (Jer. 17:9). By nature and by action, the sinner is at enmity with God.

Isaiah 53:6 says, "We all, like sheep, have gone astray, each of us has turned to his own way." The fact that man today looks up and says no to God is evidence that man is at enmity with God. Man lives for the world and the flesh; his motive is self-glory. He is interested only in pleasing himself; he is not interested in glorifying God. The Word of God tells us that friendship with the world is enmity with God (see James 4:4); and of course, the unsaved person lives for the world and the things of the world.

More than that, the unsaved person often brags about his own self-righteousness. "The sinful mind is hostile to God" (Rom. 8:7). Men boast of their own goodness! So the sinner is at war with God, and if he stays at war with God, he will die and be separated from God throughout all eternity.

THE SAVIOR

This is where reconciliation comes in. The Savior is the second Person involved in the work of reconciliation. He loves and reconciles lost sinners. God did not need to be reconciled to man. It was Adam who ran from God, not God who ran from Adam. When man sinned against God, God went and sought man. God called to Adam, "Where are you?" (Gen. 3:9). God never forsakes man. This is very important to remember. If God were to forsake you for an instant, you would die, for "in him we live and move and have our being" (Acts 17:28). So God did not need to be reconciled to man; it is man who needs to be reconciled to God.

This is why God sent His Son, the Lord Jesus Christ. "But God demonstrates his own love for us in this: While we were still sinners, Christ died for us" (Rom. 5:8). God *proved* His love toward us. The proof of God's love is not seen in nature or in history, although we can see Him there. The proof is at Calvary, on the cross where Christ died for our sins.

God hates sin, but God loves the sinner. The more you love someone, the more you despise the bad things they do. Every parent knows this. You love your son or daughter, but you hate the things they do that wreck their lives. God loves lost sinners, and the more sinners rebel against God, the more they sin against the love of God. This is why the Savior came to die.

Obstacles to Reconciliation

There are some obstacles to reconciliation. In our human life we may reconcile people who are at war with each other and not really solve the problem. Some reconciliation is only a truce, and it doesn't last. God doesn't work that way. God is concerned with removing the obstacles that stand between Him and the sinner He loves.

Of course, the first obstacle is God's holy Law. God cannot break His own Law. "The soul who sins is the one who will die" (Ezek. 18:4). "Consecrate yourselves and be holy, because I am holy" (Lev. 11:44). God's holy Law stands between the sinner and heaven.

Second, there is human guilt. God just can't take the record He has of our guilt and destroy it. God knows what is going on. He watches, and He judges. Nothing can be hidden from His eyes. You may think you are hiding something from God, but God knows all about it. God's holy Law stands between the sinner and God. Guilt stands between the sinner and God. And third, our selfish nature stands between us and God. At heart we are rebels. If there is going to be reconciliation, God has to do something about His Law, about our guilt, and about our selfish, sinful nature.

Of course, people try to solve the problem themselves. We lower the standard and say, "Well, I'm as good as anybody else. My guilt is not too bad. I'll just start all over again." But even if we did start all over again today, what about our past record of guilt? We cannot change our own hearts. That heart can be changed only by God.

Removal of the Obstacles

Jesus Christ removed all of these obstacles. He satisfied the holy demands of God's Law. We have already discussed this in our study of propitiation. When our Lord died on the cross, He met the demands of God's holy Law.

Second, He bore the guilt of our sins on the cross. This is justification. In other words, we can stand before God in the righteousness of Christ. There is no more guilt.

Third, because of His death, burial, and resurrection, Jesus Christ can change the heart. He can give us not only a new *position*, but a new *disposition*. The Bible calls this regeneration, being born again. "God has poured out his love into our hearts by the Holy Spirit" (Rom. 5:5).

So Jesus Christ has reconciled God and man. He has removed the obstacles. The Law has been satisfied, the guilt has been paid for, and the heart can be changed through the power of Jesus Christ. Of course, the price for all of this was His death on the cross. "God made him who had no sin to be sin for us, so that in him we might become the righteousness of God" (2 Cor. 5:21). Reconciliation is not man's work, it is God's work. It is God who brings us together through Jesus Christ.

THE BELIEVER

Now let us look at the believer. What does it mean to us as believers to be reconciled? Why would an unbeliever even want to be reconciled?

Let me make it very clear that reconciliation is not merely a second chance. If it were only a second chance, then the next time you sinned, you would be lost. Reconciliation is not a temporary truce. God doesn't change; God doesn't lie. What God does, He does permanently. Reconciliation is a permanent bringing together of the believing sinner and God through Jesus Christ.

I would remind you that the cross is a plus sign, and a plus sign brings things together. Romans 5:10 says, "For if, when we were God's enemies, we were reconciled to him through the death of his Son, how much more, having been reconciled, shall we be saved through his life!" Romans 5 uses the phrase "much more" several times. Reconciliation gives you "much more."

Now that we are His children, we have security. We are justified by His blood. Nothing can change that. We have victory. We can "reign in life through the one man, Jesus Christ" (see v. 17). If He did so much for us by His death, how much more He can do for us in His life. We are not only saved by His death, but we are also saved by His life—

saved from defeat, saved from future wrath. "Since we have now been justified by his blood, how much more shall we be saved from God's wrath through him!" (v. 9). So we have security, we have victory, we have sufficiency. All that we need, God gives to us. Romans 5:21 says, "Just as sin reigned in death, so also grace might reign through righteousness to bring eternal life through Jesus Christ our Lord." God takes rebels and makes kings out of them. God takes slaves and makes sovereigns out of them. That is reconciliation.

Along with reconciliation comes responsibility. We are ambassadors for Christ. The world we live in is at war with God. Sinners need to be reconciled to God. God is already reconciled—God has turned His face toward us. Now it is our task to spread the Good News, to tell people they don't have to be at war with God because God is not at war with them.

This is a day of God's grace. There is coming a day of judgment, and then it will be too late. What a privilege it is to be an ambassador for Jesus Christ—wherever you are— at home, in your neighborhood, at work, at school. What good news we have—the Good News of reconciliation.

10

Redemption

SET FREE FROM BONDAGE

FREEDOM IS a precious commodity in today's world. Each year more and more people lose their personal freedom. An organization called Freedom House monitors this situation, and they now report that not all the people in the world are truly free.

Freedom was a precious commodity in the New Testament world. One specialist tells us there were at least 60 million slaves in the Roman Empire. Ancient society was built on the foundation of slavery. There were, at one time, nearly half a million slaves in the city of Corinth alone. And so the word *redemption* brought great joy and hope to these people.

Redemption is a key word in the Bible and a key word in the Christian life. It means "to purchase and set free by paying a price." That payment, of course, was the blood of Jesus Christ. "In him we have redemption through his blood" (Eph. 1:7). Jesus died on the cross that we might be redeemed. He purchased us and set us free by paying a price.

From what kind of bondage have we been freed because we have trusted Christ as our Savior? There are four different kinds of bondage from which we have been set free, and we want to examine them.

BONDAGE TO SIN

First of all, we are freed from bondage to sin. Titus 2:11–14:

> For the grace of God that brings salvation has appeared to all men. It teaches us to say "No" to ungodliness and worldly passions, and to live self-controlled, upright and godly lives in this present age, while we wait for the blessed hope—the glorious appearing of our great God and Savior, Jesus Christ, who gave himself for us to redeem us from all wickedness and to purify for himself a people that are his very own, eager to do what is good.

We have been redeemed from bondage to sin.

This, of course, reminds us of Israel in Egypt. They were in bondage. They had to answer to taskmasters. Day after day they slaved and were not paid for it. Day after day they labored and were mistreated. It was terrible bondage.

You can't convince unsaved people that they are in bondage, because they think they are free. This is part of the deceitfulness of sin. Sin promises freedom but always brings slavery. Sin promises joy and ultimately brings pain. Sin promises success, but ultimately it brings failure. The prodigal son wanted to be free. He wanted to get away from his big brother and his father, so he went out into a far country. He thought he was free, but he discovered his freedom soon turned into bondage. Not only did he become a slave of a Gentile taskmaster, but he became a servant of the pigs.

You and I, before we were saved, were not in much better shape. Titus 3:3 says, "At one time we too were foolish, disobedient, deceived and enslaved by all kinds of passions and pleasures. We lived in malice and envy, being hated and hating one another." That doesn't sound like freedom, does it?

But when God's grace appeared in Jesus Christ, we were set free. It was nothing we did ourselves; He did it for us. Titus 3:4–5 says, "But when the kindness and love of God our Savior appeared, he saved us, not because of righteous things we had done, but because of his mercy." We have been redeemed from bondage to sin, and this redemption leads to reformation. Not only do we have freedom from the guilt and the penalty of sin, but we also have freedom *not to sin,* through the power of the Holy Spirit. We have a blessed new hope: "We wait for the blessed hope—the glorious appearing of our great God and Savior, Jesus Christ" (2:13).

Have you been set free, or redeemed, from bondage to sin?

BONDAGE TO THE OLD LIFE

The second kind of bondage from which we have been redeemed is bondage to the old life. First Peter 1:18–19 says, "For you know that it was not with perishable things such as silver or gold that you were redeemed from the empty way of life handed down to you from your forefathers, but with the precious blood of Christ, a lamb without blemish or defect." The blood of Jesus Christ has set us free from bondage to the old life.

It is interesting the way Peter described this old life: "You were redeemed from the empty way of life handed down to you from your forefathers." In 1 Peter 4:2–4, Peter described this further:

> As a result, he does not live the rest of his earthly life for evil human desires, but rather for the will of God. For you have spent enough time in the past doing what pagans choose to do—living in debauchery, lust, drunkenness, orgies, carousing and detestable idolatry. They think it strange that you do not plunge with them into the same flood of dissipation, and they heap abuse on you.

The life we used to live was a life of vanity. We thought it was a life of pleasure! Unsaved people sometimes say, "Oh, you Christians don't know what it is to really enjoy life! I am free! I am doing my own thing!" The Bible describes what they are doing: "debauchery, lust, drunkenness, orgies, carousing and detestable idolatry"—a flood of dissipation (v. 3). This doesn't sound like freedom to me. The sad thing is that many people think because they are doing their own thing, they are free. True freedom is doing the will of God.

People have the idea that the will of God is bondage. It is not bondage; the will of God is beautiful freedom. When the Lord Jesus Christ saves us, He saves us and redeems us from bondage to the old life. We must not live the rest of our lives the way we used to live.

How long will the rest of our lives be? We don't know; nobody knows. We may have many years, or we may have many days. We could be called home to glory before the day ends. We don't know. "Man is destined to die once, and after that to face judgment" (Heb. 9:27). It is an appointment, not an accident, and God knows when it is going to be.

When you are redeemed, you are set free from bondage to the old life. This is why Ephesians 5:16 tells us to redeem the time. Don't live the rest of your life the way you used to live. You have been set free from that. "The old has gone, the new has come!" (2 Cor. 5:17). Therefore, redeem the time, buy up the opportunity, make the most of the rest of your life.

I would like to apply that, if I may. Perhaps you are born again, but you are following the traditions of other people. You are doing what everybody else does. Why don't you ask God what *He* wants you to do with the rest of your life? Perhaps you are in the wrong school, and you ought to be in another school training to serve God. Perhaps you are pursuing the wrong career. Perhaps you are a successful businessman, but God is calling you into His service. You could use your experience and your gifts to glorify God in full-time Christian service. If you knew you had only ten years left to live or one year left to live, how would it change your life? We should be living each day as though it were our last. We are redeemed from bondage to sin; we are redeemed from bondage to the old life. We should live wholly for God.

BONDAGE TO THE LAW

We are also redeemed from bondage to the Law. Galatians 3:13 says, "Christ redeemed us from the curse of the law by becoming a curse for us, for it is written: 'Cursed is everyone who is hung on a tree.'" Galatians 4:4–5 says, "But when the time had fully come, God sent his Son, born of a woman, born under law, to redeem those under law, that we might receive the full rights of sons."

The Law was never given to save anybody; the Law was given to reveal sin. The Law is a mirror. You don't wash your face in the mirror; you examine your face in the mirror. If you discover your face is dirty, then you need to wash your face. When you and I look into God's holy Law, we see how sinful we are, and the Law pronounces a curse. Galatians 3:10 says, "All who rely on observing the law are under a curse, for it is written: 'Cursed is everyone who does not continue to do everything written in the Book of the Law.'"

There are two very important facts in this verse. First, if you are going to be saved by the Law, you have to keep *all* of it. You can't pick and choose. It is not *à la carte*. God puts the meal in front of you and says, "This is it! You have to obey all of the Law. You can't pick and choose."

Second, you have to *continue* to obey it. If you disobey once, you are under a curse. The Word of God makes it very clear that the Law brings condemnation, not salvation. The Old Testament Jew was under Law; he had to keep certain days as special days. He had to avoid certain foods and certain places. He had to go through certain ceremonial rituals. We have been redeemed from the Law and from the curse of the Law. Galatians 5:1 says, "Stand firm, then, and do not let yourselves be burdened again by a yoke of slavery."

This does not make us lawless. The Law of God is written in our hearts by the Holy Spirit. We obey God's Law because we love God. We obey God's Law because our new nature impels us to obey God's Law. The old nature knows no Law; the new nature needs no Law. There never was a Law given that could change or control the old nature. Jesus Christ has redeemed us from the curse of the Law. "Therefore, there is now no condemnation for those who are in Christ Jesus" (Rom. 8:1).

BONDAGE TO BODIES OF SIN

We are also redeemed from bondage to our bodies of sin. This hasn't happened yet, but it is going to happen.

In Romans 8:23 we read: "We wait eagerly for our adoption as sons, the redemption of our bodies." Ephesians 1:13–14 tells us that the Holy Spirit has sealed us unto the day of redemption. Ephesians 4:30 says, "And do not grieve the Holy Spirit of God, with whom you were sealed for the day of redemption." There is coming a day of redemption.

Today our spirits have been redeemed, but our bodies have not. Our bodies are still subject to sickness and pain, accident and illness. Our bodies still experience decay. But one day we are going to see Jesus Christ and have glorified bodies. "But our citizenship is in heaven. And we eagerly await a Savior from there, the Lord Jesus Christ, who, by the power that enables him to bring everything under his control, will transform our lowly bodies so that they will be like his glorious body" (Phil. 3:20–21). We are looking forward to a glorious day of redemption.

Jesus Christ has redeemed us from sin. He has redeemed us from the old life. He has redeemed us from the Law. And He will one day come and redeem us from these bodies of sin that create so much trouble for us.

This redemption that we have is not temporary. The word *redemption* means to purchase out of the slave market and set free, never to become a slave again. A man could purchase a slave and *keep* him a slave. Jesus didn't do that. Our Lord Jesus has purchased us by His blood and set us free to glorify Him.

Hebrews 9:12 tells us that Jesus Christ is the author of eternal redemption. How long are we redeemed? For eternity. It is *eternal* redemption. We have been delivered from the power of darkness, we have been translated into the kingdom of God's dear Son (Col. 1:13–14). If you are redeemed through faith in Christ, rejoice. Rejoice in your freedom in Christ, and use that freedom to serve others and glorify the Lord Jesus Christ.

11

Intercession

CARING AND PRAYING

LONELINESS IS becoming a real problem today in spite of
the population explosion and all the media available.
Loneliness is the feeling that nobody thinks about you or
cares about you. Loneliness is not the same as solitude.
Solitude is good for us; it helps to build us up. Even our
Lord Jesus Christ came away from the crowd and enjoyed
fellowship with God in solitude. Loneliness tears us down.
Loneliness is that awful feeling down inside that you don't
count and that if you were missing nobody would miss
you. Of course, the result of loneliness is often physical
illness, emotional problems, spiritual problems, and sometimes rebellion, withdrawal, even suicide.

The wonderful message of the gospel is that the Father cares for us and that Jesus cares. We as believers ought to care. This is where intercession comes in. The truth of intercession proves that God is for us and we need not feel alone or afraid. To intercede means to act between parties to bring them together, and togetherness is the opposite of loneliness.

I would like to discuss with you a threefold intercession that is found in the Bible. And if we will understand this threefold intercession, we can never really be lonely again.

JESUS CARES AND INTERCEDES

First of all, Jesus cares and intercedes for us. Romans 8:34 says, "Who is he that condemns? Christ Jesus, who died—more than that, who was raised to life—is at the right hand of God and is also interceding for us." Today in heaven the Lord Jesus Christ is interceding for His people. When He was here on earth, He had a prayer life that touched the lives of many people. In fact, when He was dying on the cross, He prayed, "Father, forgive them, for they do not know what they are doing" (Luke 23:34). The prophet Isaiah prophesied that Jesus Christ would make intercession for the transgressors (see Isa. 53:12), and He did.

Today the Lord Jesus Christ is not praying for a lost world. That comes as a surprise to some people, but it is true. "I am not praying for the world," He said in John 17:9. Rather, He is praying for His own here on earth, and He is interceding for us in a twofold way—as our Advocate and as our High Priest.

The ministry of our Lord Jesus Christ in heaven as the Advocate is described in 1 John 2:1: "My dear children, I write this to you so that you will not sin. But if anybody does sin, we have one who speaks to the Father in our defense [an advocate]—Jesus Christ, the Righteous One."

The word translated "advocate" means a counsel for the defense. It means one who lends his presence to his friends. The Lord Jesus Christ in heaven represents us before the throne of God. This does not mean that God the Father is against us. It simply means that we ourselves cannot approach a holy God in our own name or with our own merits. We come through the merits of Jesus Christ.

As our Advocate, or Intercessor, the Lord Jesus Christ restores us when we have sinned. It is true that we shouldn't sin, but we do. Each of us faces temptation, and sometimes we fall. John said, "Get up, confess that sin, and your Advocate will restore you." "If we confess our sins, he is faithful and just and will forgive us our sins and purify us from all unrighteousness" (1 John 1:9).

But as our High Priest, the Lord Jesus Christ intercedes to keep us from sinning. It really isn't necessary for us to sin. When we are tempted, we can come to our heavenly Intercessor, our High Priest, and He can give us the strength and grace that we need.

> Therefore, since we have a great high priest who has gone through the heavens, Jesus the Son of God, let us hold firmly to the faith we profess. For we do not have a high priest who is unable to sympathize with our weaknesses, but we have one who has been tempted in every way, just as we are—yet was without sin. Let us then approach the throne of grace with confidence, so that we may receive mercy and find grace to help us in our time of need.
>
> HEBREWS 4:14–16

Our Lord Jesus Christ cares and intercedes for us in heaven.

He knows our weaknesses, and He knows our temptations. Jesus Christ has suffered every kind of testing you and I will ever face. In fact, He endured far more, because

He was perfect. You and I do not have the kind of sensitivity that He had when He was here on earth, living in a perfect body. Jesus Christ has been through fires that we will never see. He has carried burdens that we will never feel, and He has succeeded. In heaven today He prays for us, He intercedes for us, and therefore He is able to help us succeed.

Hebrews 7:25 says, "Therefore he is able to save completely those who come to God through him, because he always lives to intercede for them." We are saved eternally, we have security, because Jesus is ever living to represent us in heaven. Jesus cares and intercedes.

The Holy Spirit Cares and Intercedes

Second, the Holy Spirit cares and intercedes. Romans 8:26 says, "In the same way, the Spirit helps us in our weakness." What is our weakness? "We do not know what we ought to pray for, but the Spirit himself intercedes for us with groans that words cannot express. And he who searches our hearts knows the mind of the Spirit, because the Spirit intercedes for the saints in accordance with God's will" (vv. 26–27).

The Holy Spirit dwells within the body of each believer. Romans 8:9 tells us very clearly that unless we have the Holy Spirit we are not saved: "And if anyone does not have the Spirit of Christ, he does not belong to Christ." The Holy Spirit lives in us, and He intercedes for us. The Holy Spirit knows the mind of the Father. A beautiful relationship is described here. The Holy Spirit intercedes for us on earth, and Jesus Christ intercedes for us in heaven. Is it any wonder that the devil attacks us? And the greatest wonder of all is that we should fall when we have this kind of assistance to see us through to victory.

Jude 1:20 tells us we should be praying in the Holy Spirit. I believe the biblical pattern for prayer is that we pray to the Father, through the Son, and in the Holy Spirit. Many times the Spirit of God will guide you to pray about something. I have been awakened at night or early in the morning with an impression upon my mind and heart that I should pray about something. And so I have prayed about it. Then I tried to remember when that time was, and I have checked afterward and often discovered that the person for whom I was praying was going through a difficult time.

I'm sure people have been stirred by the Spirit to pray for me. It's a marvelous thing to share in the intercessory work of the Holy Spirit, for the Spirit helps us to pray in the will of God. "And we know that in all things God works for the good of those who love him, who have been called according to his purpose" (Rom. 8:28). As the Holy Spirit directs us, we fulfill the purpose of God.

BELIEVERS SHOULD CARE AND INTERCEDE

Third, you and I as believers should care and intercede. "I urge, then, first of all, that requests, prayers, intercession and thanksgiving be made for everyone—for kings and all those in authority, that we may live peaceful and quiet lives in all godliness and holiness. This is good, and pleases God our Savior, who wants all men to be saved and to come to a knowledge of the truth" (1 Tim. 2:1–4). Verse 8 says, "I want men everywhere to lift up holy hands in prayer, without anger or disputing."

In the Bible you find a number of great people who were intercessors who stood between God and man and prayed. Abraham was a great intercessor. Had it not been for Abraham's prayers, Lot would never have been delivered from Sodom. Abraham knew how to intercede.

Moses was a great intercessor. Moses met God on the mountaintop and interceded for the children of Israel. In fact, he offered himself to die on their behalf.

Daniel was a great man of intercession, and so were Ezra and Nehemiah. So was the apostle Paul. Paul said his heart was just breaking because of the spiritual needs of his people, the Israelites. So when you intercede, you are a part of a great company of people; and of course, the greatest of all was our Lord Jesus Christ.

For whom should we pray? For all men, and that means all people! We should pray for those who are sick and for those who are well, for those who have problems and for those who don't have problems. We must pray for the saved and the unsaved. We should pray for "all those in authority" (v. 2). Pray for the president, for the governor of your state, for the mayor, for those who are in places of leadership. For what purpose? "That we may live peaceful and quiet lives in all godliness and holiness" (v. 2). I really believe that if Christians interceded more for people in public life, the streets would be safer and we would have better enforcement of the laws. We are to intercede for people in authority.

Certainly we are supposed to intercede for those who are lost, for God "wants all men to be saved" (v. 4). I have heard people say, "We aren't told to pray for lost sinners." But I think we are. I think if God wants *all people* to be saved and come to the knowledge of the truth and we are supposed to pray for *all people,* then we ought to pray for the lost. Do you have a list of lost people for whom you pray?

Of course, we have to have the right conditions in our own lives. First Timothy 2:8 says, "I want men everywhere to lift up holy hands in prayer, without anger or disputing." This means that we should be living a pure life, a life of fellowship and love, a life without dissention. We should be peace-loving people; we should be peacemakers, not troublemakers. We should have clean hands and a pure heart, and we should be interceding in the will of God.

Intercession is a tremendous privilege. I trust that each day you get alone with God and have before you the Word of God and perhaps a list of people about whom you are concerned. The interesting thing is this: You cannot pray for people very much without getting interested in them and learning to love them and wanting to do something for them. Prayer is really dangerous, because the more you pray, the more you are going to get involved. One of the best ways to cure loneliness is to pray and to get involved.

I trust you are praying for the pastor of your church, for your Sunday school teachers, and for the spiritual leaders in your church. I trust that God is using you to intercede. Jesus cares and intercedes. As our Advocate, He restores us; and as our High Priest, He strengthens us to keep us from sinning. The Holy Spirit cares and intercedes. He guides us in the will of God and helps us to pray in the will of God as we surrender to Him. And you and I should care and intercede.

Don't ever say to somebody, "Well, the least I can do is pray for you." My friend, the *most* you can do is pray, because intercession has great power, and intercession is a great privilege.

12

Mediation

SETTLING ENMITY

"FOR THERE IS one God and one mediator between God and men, the man Christ Jesus" (1 Tim. 2:5). In these days of international conferences and difficult problems, we frequently hear the word *mediation*. A mediator is someone who seeks to bring two or more opposing parties together in some kind of agreement.

In the New Testament world, a mediator was a neutral party that both sides could trust—an umpire or a negotiator who would not only establish peaceful relationships between the parties, but also guarantee the terms of the agreement. First Timothy 2:5 tells us that Jesus Christ is a mediator. You will notice that "mediation" is found in the context of the doctrine of intercession because intercession and mediation go together.

What is mediation? Mediation is the ministry of Jesus Christ in bringing God and man together and settling the enmity once and for all. First Timothy 2:6 says, "Who gave himself as a ransom for all men."

A QUALIFIED MEDIATOR

Is Jesus Christ qualified to be a mediator? He certainly is.

Qualified in His Person

To begin with, He is qualified in His person. He is both God and man, which is important. A mediator must be able to understand both parties. Jesus Christ, in His person, is a perfect mediator because He is God and He is man. "For there is one God and one mediator between God and men, the man Christ Jesus" (1 Tim. 2:5). But this man Christ Jesus is also God.

It never ceases to amaze me how people can read the New Testament and come to the conclusion that Jesus is not God. The demons announced that He was God. He Himself claimed to be God. In fact, when He was under oath in the Jewish court, He said that He was God. The entire Bible bears witness to the fact that Jesus Christ is God.

When He came to earth, Jesus became man—sinless man, sympathetic man. When He was here on earth, our Lord Jesus went through every testing that anybody could experience, and he came out victorious. He was "holy, blameless, pure, set apart from sinners" (Heb. 7:26), and yet He was the friend of publicans and sinners.

In the Old Testament, the prophets were not mediators. The prophets did not stand between God and man and try to bring the two together. They announced what God had given them to announce. They were God's spokesmen. The priests were not really mediators, because they themselves had to have a sacrifice for their own sins. They certainly could not bring God and man together permanently, because nothing the Old Testament priests did was permanent. It was not until the Lord Jesus Christ came that the matter was settled completely. The Old Testament prophets could preach the Word, and the priests could carry on the ceremonies, but they could not permanently settle the problem of the enmity between God and man.

Qualified in His Death

Jesus Christ is not only qualified to be a mediator in His person, but He is qualified to be a mediator in His death. His death makes possible the removal of the enmity between God and man. "[He] gave himself as a ransom for all men" (1 Tim. 2:6).

This matter is dealt with in Hebrews 9:13–16:

> The blood of goats and bulls and the ashes of a heifer sprinkled on those who are ceremonially unclean sanctify them so that they are outwardly clean. How much more, then, will the blood of Christ, who through the eternal Spirit offered himself unblemished to God, cleanse our consciences from acts that lead to death, so that we may serve the living God! For this reason Christ is the mediator of a new covenant, that those who are called may receive the promised eternal inheritance—now that he has died as a ransom to set them free from the sins committed under the first covenant. In the case of a will, it is necessary to prove the death of the one who made it.

Under the Old Covenant there were various ceremonies. The priests would shed the blood of animals and sprinkle it according to God's directions. They had special "holy water" made of the ashes of a heifer that had been offered. These various ceremonies gave outward sanctification—they dealt with sin in a ceremonial way, but they could not change the heart.

If the blood of bulls and goats and the holy water that was sprinkled in the Old Testament era purified the flesh (outward sanctification), how much more shall the blood of Jesus Christ cleanse us? The blood of Jesus Christ works in the conscience and in the heart and takes away sin. "For this reason Christ is the mediator of a new covenant" (v. 15). In His work the Lord Jesus Christ is the perfect mediator. As it were, when He was nailed to the cross, with one arm He reached up to heaven and touched God, and with the other arm He reached down to a needy world and touched sinners and brought the two together.

Qualified in His Present Ministry

Jesus Christ's present ministry in heaven today qualifies Him to be a mediator. Hebrews 8:6 says, "But the ministry Jesus has received is as superior to theirs as the covenant of which he is mediator is superior to the old one, and it is founded on better promises."

The Old Testament high priest was not a mediator in the same sense as our Lord Jesus Christ. The Old Covenant was a covenant of legal works; the New Covenant is one of faith and grace. The Old Covenant was external with washings and sacrifices, which could only deal with external uncleanness. The New Covenant is internal: It deals with the inner life of the person—the heart, the conscience. Under the Old Covenant nothing was finished, but the New Covenant is completed. Jesus said, "It is finished" (John 19:30), and He is the guarantee that this covenant is going to stand.

In the New Testament world, a mediator not only brought people together, but also guaranteed the terms of the agreement. He would see to it that the terms of the agreement were met. In Hebrews 7:22 the Lord Jesus Christ is called the guarantee of a better covenant. As long as He is alive in heaven, you and I have eternal salvation. "Therefore he is able to save completely those who come to God through him, because he always lives to intercede for them" (v. 25). He is the mediator in His present ministry, and He is all that we need.

DEFINITION OF MEDIATION

As I have said, mediation is the ministry of Jesus Christ in bringing God and man together and settling the enmity once and for all, guaranteeing the terms of the agreement so that we are saved eternally.

Not a Truce

Let's consider what mediation is not. It is not declaring a truce. A truce can always end. Genesis 31 tells the story of Laban and Jacob, two of the biggest schemers found anywhere in Scripture. It is difficult to know who was the better schemer. Jacob had run away and taken his family with him. Laban chased him, caught up with him, and started an argument. They needed some kind of agreement. So they put up a heap of stones, and this heap of stones was called "Mizpah" (vv. 48–49), meaning "watchtower." "May the LORD keep watch between you and me when we are away from each other" (v. 49). This statement is often used as a benediction, but it really should not be. Let me explain why.

Do you know what Laban and Jacob were saying to each other? They were saying, "I don't trust you, and you don't trust me, so we're going to put up this heap of stones. Laban, don't you cross over the border; Jacob, don't you cross over the border. We can't watch each other, but the Lord is going to watch, and you had better keep the terms of the agreement." What a statement to use to close a church service! "We don't trust each other, but the Lord is going to watch between us." This is just declaring a truce. These men had been at odds with each other for more than twenty years; now they said, "Let's declare a truce and get it over with."

But that is not what mediation is. Mediation doesn't just declare a truce; mediation ends the war. Mediation removes the enmity. Jesus Christ bore the wrath of God for sin. Oh, the way they mistreated Him! And yet He lovingly, willingly died for us! Now He is the mediator between God and man.

Not Arguing with God

Mediation is not declaring a truce, nor is mediation an opportunity to argue with God. In Job 9:32–33, Job cried out for an arbitrator, a mediator, somebody who would represent him so that he could argue with God. He said, "How can I prove that I am right? I can't lay hands on God; He is too far away from me. I need somebody who can lay hands upon both of us." Who in the world could ever lay hands upon God? Only God could do that. Job was here crying out for the Lord Jesus Christ, the Mediator.

So mediation is not declaring a truce, and mediation is not an opportunity to argue with God. Mediation is the ministry of Jesus Christ in bringing us together with God and keeping us together and ministering to us from heaven.

Peace with God

What does it mean in a practical way to have a mediator in heaven? First of all, it means peace with God. "Therefore, since we have been justified through faith, we have peace with God" (Rom. 5:1). We are no longer at enmity with God. Jesus Christ has brought us together, and He is keeping us together. When you have peace with God, you have peace in your heart, no matter what trials may come.

Acceptance with God

Second, it means acceptance with God. We know that we are accepted as long as Jesus Christ is alive in heaven as our mediator. There is only one God and one mediator. If there were two mediators, there wouldn't be peace. The church does not mediate between your soul and God. No religious person mediates between you and God; only Jesus Christ is the Mediator.

Access to God and Security

Third, we have access to God. Because we have a mediator in heaven, we are able to pray and intercede for others. Our intercession is based on His mediation.

Finally, it means security. We are secure because Jesus Christ, the Mediator, has finished the work. There is a beautiful picture of heaven in Hebrews 12:22: "But you have come to Mount Zion, to the heavenly Jerusalem, the city of the living God." Verse 24 says, "To Jesus the mediator of a new covenant." He is in heaven administering the terms of the New Covenant. As long as He is there, we are saved and we are secure.

It is good to know we have a mediator in heaven. Mediation is something you and I cannot do. Intercession is something we can share in, but not mediation. We can't come between God and man and settle the problem. We can pray and we can witness, but Jesus Christ is the only mediator. Jesus said, "I am the way and the truth and the life. No one comes to the Father except through me" (John 14:6).

Formed

THE BELIEVER'S HISTORY

ON THE CAPITOL DOME in Washington, D.C., you will find the following inscription: "One God, one law, one element and one supreme event toward which the whole creation moves." What is that event? The inscription doesn't tell us. Is it the destruction of the world? Is it the bringing in of a perfect society? No. That one event toward which the whole creation is moving is the coming of our Lord Jesus Christ, at which time God's people will be conformed to Jesus Christ. Romans 8:29 says, "For those God foreknew he also predestined to be conformed to the likeness of his Son."

You can summarize the history of the believer in the word *form*. We are only clay. Clay cannot form itself; only God can form us. There are four stages in the life of every child of God. First, we were *formed* in God's image by God. Second, we were *deformed* from God's image by sin. Third, we are being *transformed* into God's image by the Spirit. Fourth, we shall one day be *conformed* to the Lord Jesus Christ when we see Him.

FORMED IN GOD'S IMAGE

Let's examine this first stage in our spiritual experience: We were formed in God's image by God. "The LORD God formed the man from the dust of the ground and breathed into his nostrils the breath of life, and the man became a living being" (Gen. 2:7). "So God created man in his own image, in the image of God he created him; male and female he created them" (1:27). What does it mean to be formed in God's image? It does not mean physical likeness, because God is a spirit and does not have a body like we do. Some false religions try to teach us that God is physical and that man can one day become like God in that respect. The image of God means that we, like God, are a trinity—spirit, soul, and body. God is a Trinity—Father, Son, and Holy Spirit.

Personality

But the image of God means even more than that. It means personality. God is a person. God has a mind to think with, a heart to feel with, and a will for decisions and action. Our personality is a reflection of the personality of God. Man is basically spiritual. In his material body, man is related to the earth; he came from dust. But in his spiritual makeup, he is related to God. He is both dust and deity, so to speak. We have both heaven and earth in our makeup, and God made us this way. We were formed in God's image by God.

This is an important doctrine in the Bible, and it has some very practical applications. If we were formed in God's image by God, then we have dignity—we are not just animals. Some people live like animals, and this is too bad, but we are not animals. Man began with dignity, created by God in His image. This means that human life is valuable.

It is inconsistent for people who do not believe we were created by God in His image to want to exalt man. If man is just an animal, then why not let him live like an animal? Why have standards? Why have laws? Why does society need protection if we are only animals? It is inconsistent. The fact that we are made in God's image means we have dignity. We are not just animals.

Responsibility

Being made in the image of God means we have responsibility. We are responsible to God. He is the Creator, and we are the creatures. The way you treat other people is a reflection of what you think about God, because man was made in the image of God. We have no right to abuse or exploit other people, because they too were made in the image of God.

Destiny

Being made in God's image means we have a special destiny. We were created by God in His image for a definite purpose. We are not here by accident; we are here by appointment. We are here to glorify God and to enjoy Him forever, as the catechism tells us. This explains why many people have such empty lives today. They don't realize this dignity, they don't fulfill this responsibility, and they are not prepared for this marvelous destiny.

DEFORMED FROM GOD'S IMAGE

If we were formed in God's image by God, why then is everything in such a mess? Well, because we were deformed from God's image by sin. How else can you explain the chaos the world is in today? Something in us cries out for God, and something else in us cries out for sin. Why is that? Because man fell, man is a sinner. When man fell into sin, his spirit died—he was separated from God. His soul was damaged; the image of God in him was damaged by sin. We no longer possess the kind of faculties that God gave us in the beginning. Something tragic has happened.

Ephesians 4:18–19 says, "They are darkened in their understanding and separated from the life of God because of the ignorance that is in them due to the hardening of their hearts. Having lost all sensitivity, they have given themselves over to sensuality so as to indulge in every kind of impurity, with a continual lust for more." This is the result of sin. We were deformed from God's image by sin. The spirit died, and the soul has been damaged. The mind no longer thinks God's thoughts, the heart no longer loves God, the will is no longer submitted to God.

Of course, one day the body will die. God said to Adam and Eve, "For when you eat of it you will surely die" (Gen. 2:17). This is where death came from. We came from the dust, we are going back to the dust, and we cannot help ourselves. Only God can make the difference.

TRANSFORMED INTO GOD'S IMAGE

We were formed in God's image by God, and we were deformed from God's image by sin. But when we trust Jesus Christ as our Savior, a miracle takes place. Our spirits become alive again, and God begins to work on our inner beings to make us more like Himself. We are being transformed into God's image by the Spirit.

Romans 12:1–2 says,

> Therefore, I urge you, brothers, in view of God's mercy, to offer your bodies as living sacrifices, holy and pleasing to God—this is your spiritual act of worship. Do not conform any longer to the pattern of this world, but be transformed by the renewing of your mind. Then you will be able to test and approve what God's will is—his good, pleasing and perfect will.

When you trust Christ as your Savior, the Holy Spirit comes in, and you become a new creation. God starts all over again. "Therefore, if anyone is in Christ, he is a new creation; the old has gone, the new has come!" (2 Cor. 5:17).

In Colossians 3:10 Paul wrote this: "[You] have put on the new self, which is being renewed in knowledge in the image of its Creator." When you surrender to Jesus Christ as your Lord—give Him your body, your mind, your will, and your heart—God begins to transform you.

Romans 12:2 says, "Do not conform any longer to the pattern of this world, but be transformed by the renewing of your mind." The word *transformed* is the word *transfigure*. In Matthew 17 our Lord was transfigured before His disciples. Transfiguration is a change on the outside that comes from the inside. You can change the outside with a masquerade costume, but masquerading has no place in the Christian life. Transformation is a change on the outside that comes from the inside. It is the work of the Holy Spirit.

This is why we read the Bible. As we read the Word of God, the Spirit of God transforms us and renews our mind. This is why we pray. I can't explain prayer. I have read many books on prayer and have studied it, but prayer, to me, is a continuous miracle. As we pray and fellowship with God, a transformation takes place in our character. Moses went up on the mountaintop and met with God. When he came down, his face was shining, but that glory eventually faded. You and I don't borrow glory and then lose it. We have the glory down inside. We are being transformed into God's image by the Holy Spirit.

This means we are *not* conforming to the world. Christians should not love the world or try to please the world. In our body, our mind, our will, our heart, we are trying, with the help of the Holy Spirit, to be more like the Lord Jesus Christ.

CONFORMED TO GOD'S IMAGE

We were formed in God's image by God, we were deformed from God's image by sin, and we are being transformed into God's image by the Spirit. One day we will be conformed to God's image when we see Jesus Christ.

This is not some vague hope; this is an assurance based on God's Word. Romans 8:29 says, "For those God foreknew he also predestined to be conformed to the likeness of his Son." "But our citizenship is in heaven. And we eagerly await a Savior from there, the Lord Jesus Christ, who, by the power that enables him to bring everything under his control, will transform our lowly bodies so that they will be like his glorious body" (Phil. 3:20–21). One day we shall be like the Lord Jesus Christ, for we shall see Him as He is.

That is the blessed hope of the believer. In fact, we have already been glorified. Notice Romans 8:30: "And those he predestined, he also called; those he called, he also justified; those he justified, he also glorified." Glorified— already completed! Jesus said, "I have given them the glory that you gave me" (John 17:22). When we see the Lord Jesus Christ, we will be conformed to His image.

Let's not be conformed to the world. That is such a waste of time and energy, and you miss so many blessings. All history is moving in the direction of the coming of Jesus Christ. Let God transform you daily. Let the Holy Spirit use the Word of God to transform your mind. Yield to Him, and look forward to the coming of the Lord Jesus. Whatever your weaknesses and problems may be, just remember that one day you and I will be conformed to God's image when we see Jesus Christ. But let's not wait until then. Let's start being transformed by the Lord Jesus Christ today by letting the Spirit of God have His way.

14

Predestination

GOD'S PLAN FOR HIS OWN

GOD HAS MADE this universe to operate a day at a time. And you and I are supposed to live a day at a time. God's promise is that "your strength will equal your days" (Deut. 33:25). You and I are able to live a day at a time because God is in control.

Have you ever walked into a group of people in the middle of a conversation and felt uneasy because you did not know what was going on? Have you ever started to read in the middle of a book? When we walk into the middle of something, we get frustrated because we are not sure what's going on.

Many people today are not sure what is going on. Change is taking place so rapidly and so radically these days that people are afraid. Some people are even rebellious. Rebellion, after all, is fear turned inside out. Some people become sick or nervous from life's pressures and then withdraw, using their illness as an excuse. Some people even commit suicide because they cannot take the pressures of life.

For life to be meaningful, we have to know where we came from, why we are here, and where we are going. Of course, many people have philosophies that try to give those facts. The Communist talks about economic forces and class struggle. The evolutionist has his solution to the problem in his doctrine of the survival of the fittest. The agnostic says, "Well, we just don't know; we're living by chance or by luck. Enjoy today because tomorrow may not come. Do your own thing." He has a fatalistic philosophy of life. And then we have superstitious people. They study the stars, and they consult astrological charts. They might even dabble in the occult. But the Christian doesn't need any of this because the Christian has his Bible, and the Bible teaches us that God is in control.

What I want to share with you is all wrapped up in the word *predestination*. The minute you mention that word, some people get nervous because right in the middle of predestination is the word *destiny*. It sounds so fatalistic and frightening. The Christian is not afraid of life. He is not afraid to live a day at a time, because he has his confidence in God and knows that God is in control.

Romans 8:28–30 says,

And we know that in all things God works for the good of those who love him, who have been called according to his purpose. For those God foreknew he also predestined to be conformed to the likeness of his Son, that he might be the firstborn among many brothers. And those he predestined, he also called; those he called, he also justified; those he justified, he also glorified.

We have in these three verses God's wonderful plan for His people. We are going to study this word *predestinate* because when you understand it, you will be able to relax and not worry about what is going on around you.

The word *predestinate* is used only six times in the New Testament, but it is not always translated that way. It is the Greek word *prohorizo*. You say, "Well, what does that mean?" *Pro* means "beforehand," and h*orizo* means "to mark out." Our word *horizon* comes from that word. The horizon is that area marked out before us that separates the sky from the land.

Let's answer three questions about predestination, and in answering these questions, calm our fears and assure our hearts.

WHAT DOES PREDESTINATION MEAN?

Predestination is God's eternal plan to make His own children like the Lord Jesus Christ. The English prefix *pre* means "beforehand," and *destinate* means "destiny." *Pre-destination* means "a destination planned beforehand." Predestination simply affirms that God has an eternal plan for His children. The destiny He has planned for them is that they shall be like the Lord Jesus Christ. "For those God foreknew he also predestined to be conformed to the likeness of his Son" (Rom. 8:29).

You should note some important facts about predestination. First of all, predestination applies only to the saved. I do not know any place in the Bible where it says that God predestines people to go to hell. I do not find any place in the Word of God where we are told that God predestines people to be lost. Quite the contrary is true. He tells us to go into *all* the world and preach the gospel.

Does the Bible teach election? It certainly does. "For he chose us in him before the creation of the world" (Eph. 1:4). Does this mean that we cannot share the gospel with everybody? No, it doesn't. You and I do not know who God's elect are. Predestination teaches us that God's elect are one day going to be like the Lord Jesus Christ.

Two contrasting verses are found in Matthew 25. Verse 34 says, "Then the King will say to those on his right, 'Come, you who are blessed by my Father; take your inheritance, the kingdom prepared for you since the creation of the world.'" In verse 41 we read: "Then he will say to those on his left, 'Depart from me, you who are cursed, into the eternal fire prepared for the devil and his angels.'" Verse 41 does not say, "Prepared for you from before the foundation of the world." But He did say to the saved that the kingdom had been prepared for them from the foundation of the world.

Predestination comes from the heart of a loving Father. We must never think of predestination as some cold program that God worked out in the distant glories of eternity. Ephesians 1:4–5 says, "For he chose us in him before the creation of the world to be holy and blameless in his sight. In love he predestined us to be adopted as his sons." How has He predestined us? *In love.* Predestination is the wise plan of a loving Father, and He is going to work out His plan.

Something else is true. Predestination is only part of the total plan. Five key factors are mentioned in Romans 8:29–30 and we will now look at them.

How Does Predestination Work?

According to Romans 8:29 predestination begins with foreknowledge: "For those God foreknew he also predestined." Foreknowledge does not simply mean to know beforehand. There are those who teach that God knew beforehand who would believe; therefore, He predestinated them to be saved. That's backward. If God only *foresees* future events, then what makes these events certain? An event must be made certain before it can be known as certain, and only God can make events certain.

To foreknow means to choose beforehand, to set your love upon someone. This is all by God's grace. God in His grace sets His love upon certain ones who are going to be saved. That is where it all begins—with God's gracious foreknowledge. Either salvation is by grace, totally from the loving heart of God, or there is no salvation at all.

God sets His love upon certain ones. These certain ones are predestined, then, to be conformed to the image of Christ. Of course, this involved the death of Christ, and even that was predestined. Acts 4:27–28 says, "Indeed Herod and Pontius Pilate met together with the Gentiles and the people of Israel in this city to conspire against your holy servant Jesus, whom you anointed. They did what your power and will had decided beforehand should happen." The death of Christ was not an accident; it was predestined by a loving Father.

Predestination simply means that one day you are going to be like Jesus Christ. It begins with foreknowledge, and then it involves being called by the Holy Spirit. Romans 8:30 says, "And those he predestined, he also called." This calling comes through human agency.

Don't ever get the idea that because God has elected some and those whom He has elected are predestined to go to heaven, that Christians should do nothing. "But we ought always to thank God for you, brothers loved by the Lord, because from the beginning God chose you to be saved through the sanctifying work of the Spirit and through belief in the truth. He called you to this through our gospel, that you might share in the glory of our Lord Jesus Christ" (2 Thess. 2:13–14). Those whom God elects and foreknows, He predestines, and those whom He predestines, He calls. That is why we have a ministry of sharing the Word of God. That is why we witness and pray.

Those who are called are justified—declared righteous. Those whom He justified, He also glorified. Again notice the past tense of that verb: "And those he justified, he also glorified" (Rom. 8:30).

This is God's total plan. What begins with foreknowledge ends with glory. Predestination simply declares that God's people are going to make it—they will one day be conformed to the image of Christ.

WHAT DOES PREDESTINATION MEAN TODAY?

What does predestination mean to us today as believers? Please keep in mind that Paul wrote the Book of Romans to ordinary people, not theologians or philosophers. Theologians wrestle with some of these things, but Paul did not write Romans to theologians. He wrote for common people, and he knew they could understand it if they would just open their hearts to the Spirit.

Salvation Is Bigger Than We Think

First of all, predestination means that salvation is much bigger than what we think. Your salvation is not a minor incident; it is part of an eternal plan. God is so gracious that, from all eternity, He has planned that we shall be conformed to the image of His Son. Don't ever allow salvation to become a minor thing. It is a big thing, far bigger than we realize. It is a part of a great eternal plan.

God Is Bigger Than Our Trials

Second, predestination means that God is much bigger than our trials and our troubles. Notice Romans 8:31: "What, then, shall we say in response to this?" Say in response to what? The facts that we are foreknown, predestined, called, justified, and already glorified. We say, "If God is for us, who can be against us?" In the rest of Romans 8, Paul spelled out so beautifully that God is bigger than all of our sufferings and trials.

You may hurt today. Things may be falling apart today. But I want you to know that if you are saved, you are a part of something eternal and big and wonderful and glorious. God is bigger than any trouble you may go through.

No Christian Will Be Lost

Third, predestination means that no true Christian will ever be lost. There can be no separation from God. God started this great salvation, and God is going to see it to completion. God knew what was happening long before these things ever took place. I cannot believe that any true Christian can ever be lost, because all believers are a part of a great eternal plan.

God's plan of salvation was secure from all eternity. The Lamb was slain from before the foundation of the world (see Rev. 13:8). God is not caught by surprise. God is not depending on your strength or mine. "Those he justified, he also glorified" (Rom. 8:30). God is so sure we are going to heaven that He has already glorified us. All we are waiting for is the revelation of that glory.

We Live by Faith

This leads us to a fourth application: We have to live by faith, not by sight. God knows what He is doing. Jacob was walking by sight when he said, "Everything is against me!" (Gen. 42:36). Really, everything was working *for* him. So walk by faith, not by sight, and let God have His way.

We Must Obey God

Finally, we must obey God and share in His purpose. He is working out His beautiful plan in your life, so don't be afraid, and don't be alarmed. God has everything all taken care of. Just trust Him, obey Him, and walk with Him. Pray and believe, and one of these days, with all of God's people, you will end up in heaven—glorified!

15

Glorification

COMPLETION OF GOD'S PLAN

ONE BALMY SUMMER DAY my wife and I visited one of the most famous cemeteries in the world. This cemetery is located at Stoke Poges, not far from Windsor Castle in England. It was there that Thomas Gray wrote his famous poem "Elegy Written in a Country Churchyard." Perhaps you had to read that poem and memorize part of it when you were in school. As I stood there among those ancient graves, one stanza of that poem came to my mind:

> The boast of heraldry, the pomp of pow'r,
> And all that beauty, all that wealth e'er gave,
> Awaits alike the inevitable hour:
> The paths of glory lead but to the grave.

Thomas Gray was right when he wrote that. As far as man is concerned, all of his glory ends at the grave. "For you have been born again, not of perishable seed, but of imperishable, through the living and enduring word of God. For, 'All men are like grass, and all their glory is like the flowers of the field; the grass withers and the flowers fall, but the word of the Lord stands forever.' And this is the word that was preached to you" (1 Peter 1:23–25). Man's glory does not last because man's glory has been stained by sin.

Man once walked with God and shared in God's glory, but now "all have sinned and fall short of the glory of God" (Rom. 3:23). Glorification is an important doctrine in the Bible. The glory of God simply means the sum total of all that God is, the expression of His essence. Glory is the result of all that God does. Only God has glory, and only God deserves glory. But as Christians, we share in the glory of God. Romans 5:2 says, "Through [our Lord Jesus Christ] we have gained access by faith into this grace in which we now stand. And we rejoice in the hope of the glory of God." Romans 8:30 says, "Those he justified, he also glorified." You and I, as believers, share in the glory of God.

GOD COMPLETES HIS ETERNAL PLAN

What does this doctrine of glorification really mean? It means, first of all, that God completes His eternal plan. I trust that as we have been studying the key words of the Christian life, you have discovered that salvation is not some minor incident in history. Salvation is part of a great plan established from eternity. Your salvation is not an accident; your salvation is not some little thing. Your salvation is part of God's great eternal plan, and the end of that plan is glorification. "Those he justified, he also glorified" (Rom. 8:30).

In Ephesians 1, Paul reminded us three times that salvation is for God's glory: "to the praise of his glorious grace" (v. 6), "that we . . . might be for the praise of his glory" (v. 12), "who is a deposit guaranteeing our inheritance until the redemption of those who are God's possession—to the praise of his glory" (v. 14).

One of these days the Lord Jesus Christ is going to return and put everything together. The devil is busy tearing things apart, and he has a great deal of help from sinners. But one day the Lord Jesus Christ is going to put everything together. Ephesians 1:9–10 tells us "he made known to us the mystery of his will according to his good pleasure, which he purposed in Christ, to be put into effect when the times will have reached their fulfillment—to bring all things in heaven and on earth together under one head, even Christ." Jesus Christ is going to gather everything together, and we are going to enter into glory.

The greatest purpose possible in all of the universe is the glory of God, not the glory of man. Man does not have anything worth glorying about. When God does things for His own glory, He is not being selfish or egotistical. There is none higher than God; there is none greater than God. If anyone who is less than God were glorified, it would not be right. God, being as great as He is, deserves all glory and all praise and all honor.

In fact, this is what they are singing about in heaven. "You are worthy, our Lord and God, to receive glory and honor and power, for you created all things, and by your will they were created and have their being" (Rev. 4:11). Can you look at any human being and say, "You are worthy to receive glory and honor"? "In a loud voice they sang: 'Worthy is the Lamb, who was slain, to receive power and wealth and wisdom and strength and honor and glory and praise!'" (5:12). You can find no higher purpose in the universe than the glory of God. Glorification means that God completes His eternal plan.

If you are going through suffering now, I want to remind you that, according to the Bible, suffering leads to glory. "And the God of all grace, who called you to his eternal glory in Christ, after you have suffered a little while, will himself restore you" (1 Peter 5:10). "I consider that our present sufferings are not worth comparing with the glory that will be revealed in us" (Rom. 8:18). We suffer here, but it means glory over there, and God is going to compensate for all our suffering.

Keep in mind that the greatest purpose in all the world is the glory of God. Glorification means that God completes His eternal plan. Jesus didn't die just to rescue people from sin. Nor did He die on the cross just to change people's lives and put their homes back together again. He died so that God might be glorified. When you are busy in the work of evangelism, keep in mind that it is not for the purpose of counting results. It is not for the purpose of advertising statistics. It is for the purpose of glorifying God.

CHRIST IS REWARDED FOR HIS SACRIFICE

Glorification means that God completes His eternal plan. It also means that Christ is rewarded for His sacrificial work. In Jude 1:24, we read: "To him who is able to keep you from falling and to present you before his glorious presence without fault and with great joy." The Lord Jesus Christ, one of these days, is going to present His church before the Father with exceeding joy. This ties in with Hebrews 12:2: "who for the joy set before him endured the cross." What was the joy that was set before Him? The joy of one day bringing His bride to glory.

Our Lord Jesus did not only suffer physically on the cross. Other people were crucified and suffered pain. But

He also suffered *spiritually.* He was made sin for you and me. Our Lord Jesus Christ went through the agonies of hell for us. What is His reward for this? His reward is glory in the church throughout all eternity.

When our Lord Jesus Christ returns, we are going to share with Him in glory. Second Thessalonians 1:10 says, "On the day he comes to be glorified in his holy people and to be marveled at among all those who have believed." He is going to be glorified in His saints. Glorification means that God completes His eternal plan and that Christ is rewarded for His sacrificial work.

CHRISTIANS' SALVATION SHALL BE FULFILLED

Glorification also means that Christians will experience the fulfillment of their salvation. Being born again is just the beginning. When you trust Christ as your Savior, that is just the beginning—the best is yet to come!

In Romans 8:30, we discover that the ultimate experience is glorification: "Those he justified, he also glorified." Romans 8:19–23 points out the fact that, in this life, we go through trial and suffering. "The creation waits in eager expectation for the sons of God to be revealed" (v. 19). What he is saying is that all of creation is standing eagerly on tiptoe, waiting for us to be glorified. Why? Because when we are glorified, then creation will be set free from the bondage of sin. Christians will experience the fulfillment of their salvation.

To begin with, glorification means a new body. God is not saving bodies today. He is rescuing our bodies from sin, and He is using our bodies for His glory, but the major ministry God has today is not for the body. The redemption of our bodies is still in the future. God is majoring on building character, building the spiritual life to glorify God. But one day we are going to get new bodies. This corruption is going to put on incorruption, and this body of humiliation is going to put on glory. One day we will receive a glorified body like Christ's body. God saves the total person. God doesn't just save souls; God doesn't just save spirits. God saves the total person. One day we will be totally redeemed.

Glorification also means a new environment, a brand-new home. When you get discouraged, sit down and read Revelation 21 and 22. John said,

> Then I saw a new heaven and a new earth, for the first heaven and the first earth had passed away, and there was no longer any sea. I saw the Holy City, the new Jerusalem, coming down out of heaven from God, prepared as a bride beautifully dressed for her husband. And I heard a loud voice from the throne saying, "Now the dwelling of God is with men, and he will live with them. They will be his people, and God himself will be with them and be their God. He will wipe every tear from their eyes. There will be no more death or mourning or crying or pain, for the old order of things has passed away."
>
> REVELATION 21:1–4

Glorification means that we are going to enter a brand-new environment.

When God glorifies our bodies, He has to give us a glorious home to live in, and that glorious home is heaven. Heaven is a place of no pain, no death, no darkness, no sorrow, no crying. It is a place where you will never find a mortuary or a cemetery, a place where there will be no hospitals or pharmacies, a place where no tear will ever fall and no doubt will ever cloud the skies. It will be a place of glorious reunion when we meet with the Lord Jesus Christ and our loved ones who have gone before. Glorification means a new home, a new environment.

A New Ministry

And finally, glorification means a new ministry. If you have the idea that heaven is simply a place of clouds and harps and robes, you had better wake up because Revelation 7:15 tells me, "Therefore, they are before the throne of God and serve him day and night in his temple."

I don't know all that we are going to do throughout all eternity, but it is going to be wonderful. A whole universe will be opened to us. Different people have speculated about our ministry in heaven, but I am not going to speculate. All I know is that we are going to serve Him. That's why He saved us. We are going to have all eternity to grow in our knowledge of God, coming to understand His truth in a deeper way. We are going to experience the fellowship of the angels and the patriarchs and the saints of God, and we are going to enter into a new ministry. He is preparing us for our ministry now. You may wonder, "Why am I going through this time of trial?" He is preparing you for glory.

The doctrine of glorification gives me a great feeling of security. God is going to finish what He started, and God is going to glorify His church. This gives me great encouragement in times of suffering. As we go through times of difficulty, we can look up because we know Jesus is coming. We know that our suffering today is not worthy to be compared with the glory that will be revealed in us (see Rom. 8:18). To me glorification means security, encouragement in suffering, and a motivation for service.

"Therefore, my dear brothers, stand firm. Let nothing move you. Always give yourselves fully to the work of the Lord" (1 Cor. 15:58). That admonition is at the end of a great chapter on resurrection and future glory. Keep on serving. Don't give up—the best is yet to come. God's plan will be completed, and you and I will share in the total blessing of glory in heaven someday.

Warren W. Wiersbe is Distinguished Professor of Preaching at Grand Rapids Baptist Seminary and has pastored churches in Indiana, Kentucky, and Illinois (Chicago's historic Moody Church). He is the author of more than 150 books, including *God Isn't in a Hurry*, *The Bumps Are What You Climb On*, and *The Bible Exposition Commentary: New Testament* (2 vols).